SHAIDA was raised as a child in Kashmir, Pakistan. She spent the majority of her life in London, England. She was educated in London and later received a BA Honours degree after taking time out to raise a family.

Her experiences of past life are shared with the society of today.

*'So far ahead in the world we have come,
And yet, deep down inside,
We are still so far away.'*

TEARS OF SILENCE

TEARS OF SILENCE

SHAIDA MEHRBAN

ATHENA PRESS LONDON

Tears of Silence
Copyright © Shaida Mehrban 2006

All Rights Reserved

No part of this book may be reproduced in any form
by photocopying or by any electronic or mechanical means,
including information storage and retrieval systems,
without permission in writing from both the copyright
owner and the publisher of this book.

ISBN 1 84401 724 9

First Published 2006 by
ATHENA PRESS
Queen's House, 2 Holly Road
Twickenham TW1 4EG
United Kingdom

This is a true story. The names of the
characters in this book have been changed.

Printed for Athena Press

*To the memory of my much loved mother,
who in spite of being dead for more than forty years still lives
on in my heart, but more so in my head.
That inspirational one has made me write this book.
She took with her the joyful, innocent child and left behind a
child almost like Kaashi.*

One day in your care,
*   Was a lifetime of despair.*
One day without you,
*   Left me thinking why and who?*
This one day was a lifetime, full of loving,
*   This heart and soul, were never mine for giving.*
They are a piece of me, I pine,
*   For she decided this prominent fine line.*
You caressed me with your bosom and showed me happiness,
*   You heard the knock of death, but there was no forgiveness.*
The aches and pains were much too great,
*   For a lonely child to bear, with an empty life to create.*
She cut the red blood, blessed and then left me,
*   She a scorned child, for everyone to see.*
I am what's left, the remains of my mother.
*   I am what's hurting, left alone to live with another.*
So which was the greatest ado,
*   A day in the life with, or without you?*

THIS is the first in a series of true stories taken from around the world. The stories explore the lives of ordinary women within the male-dominated household, their struggles and the reality of their hardship. They share their thoughts on how they feel when coming to terms with specific compromises within their religion and culture. A struggle results when they share their frustration about their lifestyle, which demands empathy with and respect for the man because he is the dominant head of the household and keeper of the wife. At times, the only way he gains total control is through force, whether through rape, mental and domestic violence or just through his very existence.

Education, television, radio and the media have meant that women are now opening up their minds to the difference between their reality and the actual lifestyle of other women around the world. They're forced to face the unaddressed subject of oppression and inequality and the effects of these factors on them as mothers, sisters, daughters and wives.

Their own struggles have opened their eyes and minds to the fact that they want something better for their female offspring. How can their thoughts bring about change in a society that has become used to the man leading and the female following, a life where women can be seen but not heard, especially if they're speaking for equality?

These stories will not only touch the hearts of females around the world, but also the hearts of men, especially those men who respect the fact that it's a female who has given birth to them and who has helped to nurture them. Some men will feel ashamed, others will know it as reality and a few will feel pride because they have the upper hand, which means 'power'. These men also recognise that it's a female who has responded to their needs although she could be the mother, sister or daughter and later, maybe the wife of someone else.

This story begins in Kashmir in Pakistan, in the early 1960s, in an impoverished village where this male-dominated culture is very deep-rooted. The village is called Chhattro and is close to the local market area of Dadial. The nearest town is Mirpur, which is about two hours' drive away and is well known as a shopping area. Mirpur is about a two and a half hour journey away from the capital, Islamabad. This region is in the north of the country, where there is a small minority of British people and thus a Western influence.

Kaashi Sarah Khan, the main character, lives with her mother in this small, close-knit community where everyone knows everyone else. The story moves from her childhood in Pakistan to her adulthood in England. The character talks about her emotions, fears and thoughts, and the bitterness she feels towards life, which started with the death of her mother. She feels anger at being parted from her family, and is humiliated by the loss of self-respect due to years of sexual, physical and mental abuse from her own father.

It isn't just Kaashi, but also other members of the family who shed tears of silence. She tries to escape this life by getting married and ends up by being dominated by another male, this time her husband. While trying to keep her children happy and unaware of her fears, she copes with a life of domination by her partner in the hope of creating some stability and safety for them.

Whilst she is trying to cope with her own fear and anger, she also recollects stories of other females, in similar situations, who have at some point shed tears of silence.

Chapter One

'REALLY! Is it really true, Nanny Ma?'

'Yes, that's really true, little one,' came a muffled voice from the animal shed.

My head and heart were full of questions. When and how would he come? What would he be like? Would he love us? And more to the point, who would be loved more?

The stick I was holding, for hitting the goats and lambs, fell from my hand. 'What if he loves Juan more than me?' was all that kept going round in my mind. I didn't ask any more questions.

Juan is my sister; she's a year older than me. She was sensitive to many things, which meant that our nanny ma paid more attention to her. Nanny Ma was our mother's mother and our only carer since the death of our mum.

I remember that evening very well: we were sitting around the open fire, which gave us warmth and light. Winter evenings were pretty cold, so the fire was a very good idea. After all, it also served the main purpose of the day, to cook the rooster. I remember the conversation between us three. Nanny Ma assured us that everything would be fine now.

On a special occasion like today, the rooster had been caught in our courtyard, plucked, skinned, cut up and cooked over the clay fire; fresh bread was baked in a clay oven. This was a lavish lunch treat by all accounts. We both had eaten plenty, but there was still plenty left for dinner when we would be eating with our father.

This day had become quite momentous because so many

people had visited our house to wish us all the best. We were dressed in our best frocks, which showed our thin bare legs fitted into our slippers.

We asked each other many questions that had no answers: What would he be like? What would he be wearing? And so on. I certainly could never remember seeing a man around the house. We were told we could play, but not to get our dresses dirty. As usual, I had eaten too much and was told to run around and work it off. I couldn't be bothered that day, as I looked at the remains of the fire.

Would I be made to feel warm like the glowing coal or would I just be the ash on the side? Everything around me felt half numb, voices were distant, and the glow from the fire made the weight on my eyelids heavier. I listened for the sound of footsteps, but not recognisable footsteps, for these would be different. He wouldn't be wearing slippers or flip-flops like all of us!

My eyes widened, my senses awoke, and my heart fluttered as the heavy footsteps finally approached. Suddenly I looked around, forgetting to remain ladylike and pull my dress down. I was numb. Everyone and everything seemed pointless, for now and for the first time, I saw a man sitting on the big special chair for visitors, the only clean chair in the house. My sister and I got up, held hands and stood, observing.

Slowly we started muttering under our breath.
'Shall we go, Jay?'
'You go first, Kay.'
'No, you.'
'No, you.'

Chapter Two

THE excitement was immense and uncontrollable, so much so, that, rather than smiling, I was giggling excessively. His warm leg, which I was sitting on, felt soothing, and his arm was wrapped around my tiny waist, hugging me and making me feel safe. He shared his kisses equally between us both.

I looked at his hands and then looked at my own. For a girl of five I was very inquisitive. My hands were a lot smaller than his were; I still remember the fine lines on the back of his left hand, which secured me safely, like a harness. Those lines remained uppermost in my mind; they were unforgettable. No matter how much older I got, those lines remained the same in my mind, so fresh, as if I had seen them today.

Months went by and winter crept up again. We started to share our nanny ma's bed for warmth once more. During the day we would sit with our father to listen to stories; we listened with enthusiasm while replying, 'Yes, Abu.' He made sure we washed our faces, had clean clothes on, smelt nice, and ate well. The latter became a habit, as only a few days after he returned from England, we sat around the fire for our family meal together, which Nanny Ma made as usual: lamb and *roti*.

Both of us girls ate the *roti* and shared the lamb soup, trying to be extra careful not to slurp quite so loudly, leaving the meat aside. A heated debate began between the two adults sitting by the fire about how my father had sent so much money from abroad but how my nan had not spent it on feeding us well – feeding well meant eating meat.

The glow of the fire and its heat lit up their temples as well. As the flames got lower, so did their voices, and a silence and tranquillity descended. As I raised my head, which had been buried between my knees, a stream of water ran from my eyes and my nose. I wiped my face on my dress. As I lifted my eyes, a voice said, 'Eat the meat!'

These words were much harsher than the slap that was planted on my cheek. It left a lasting effect on me as I still eat meat today. As he lifted his hand from my cheek, I watched him slowly move it across the fire. As he did so, I stared at those fine lines again. Was this destiny? How could I have predicted that those fine lines would become an important part of my life?

Tears of silence ran so quickly, but no sound was heard, almost as if I was lost because of fear. I remember them as if it was yesterday. I remember how that was the beginning of 'Do as I say, or else.' We had never ever been treated like this, as our family only consisted of females: Great Grandmother Basi, Nanny Ma Sophia and Mother, Ali. They all had showered their love on the two of us.

Just love, not dominance.

Happy, not scared!

Now, just tears, tears of silence...

Chapter Three

THE monsoon rains had arrived at last, but they were very different this year. They weren't as fast or as strong. Why? Well, the previous year the ferocity had claimed a life and had unimaginably damaged our lives. The rain that had seeped through the cottage roof had had a lasting effect on our young mother. Just out of her teenage years and best suited to carry out this work, she had climbed up on the roof to repair it.

There weren't any professional builders then, so local men used to show their hidden talents when a damsel needed help. However, our mother and her mother had learnt to cope on their own. It was really late by the time mother finished and the two of us were lying on the big bed that the four of us shared, hoping for a good sleep. I still remember the final words in my ears that night: 'Leave it now, Ali. It's late and very cold, dear child. Do it tomorrow.'

Tomorrow came for everyone else, but for us everything had stopped during the night. When I awoke that morning it was almost as if the sweet voices of the birds and the loud shrills of the cockerels had all been deafened by faint, terrible screams of horror. I opened my eyes and looked straight up at the ceiling. Had it collapsed? Was I asleep amongst the ruins? I looked around to find my sister to save her. She wasn't there!

I looked at where the noise was coming from. Juan was standing on the floor, crying gently. Nanny Ma was crying loudly, beating her hands on her knees, and wiping her face with her scarf. For the rest of the day a lot of tears were shed.

People came and went; the burial and the wake ended the sorrowful day. How quickly it all happened, and no one's feelings were taken into account.

Was God really the judge that day, overruling our happiness? No one had even asked the jury for their verdict.

As I think back to that day I often wonder if it was meant to make us grow up suddenly, to be more independent so we could stick up for ourselves. Or was it for us to become weakened by the strains of a life yet to be endured? I still see that day through my heavy eyelids, full of agony and pain: an unfulfilled life and the cruel snatching away of a loved one whom a child should never be without. All those emotions pour out in my tears of silence, but who will hear me cry?

The only possible person, our mother, who we called *Ami*, had already been relieved of that responsibility. We girls were the only hope of keeping her name alive, and of course the annual feast when local people gathered and recited prayers for the young dead female. Nothing more. No questioning, just an acceptance, especially from the men in our society. How quickly they get rid of the old and invite the new! Who could take her place? No one! How easy it is for men, but how hard it is for us young ones. No mother. No love. No cuddles, no kisses. Pain, abuse, hurt and tears – lots of them.

Lots of tears, yes, tears of silence.

Chapter Four

PLANS were being made to ensure that we quickly left Pakistan for the land of hope, England. They always muttered about the four of us going together. Juan and I didn't want any more changes in our lives. This talk didn't stimulate our minds at all, but we were happy enough to accept that we were leaving the land and home only, and even though we had laid the dead one to rest, at least we would be together with our nanny ma.

We would often blank out this debate and run off into the fields where everything felt much better. We would sit perched on a tree with our friends showing no ladylike manners at all. Thin, long, bare legs descending from bare bottoms. We boasted about our new venture as somehow it lessened our pain. There was no excitement in our hearts but there was on our friends' faces. They were excited for us, and envious as well.

They called us the lucky girls, often saying, 'Lucky Jay and Kay'. How wrong they were. They still had a mother; we didn't. They shared her warmth; we couldn't. But at least we shared someone's – our nanny ma's – and that was good enough. It had to be enough!

The morning dawned. We were both asked if we wanted to go. 'Where?' Juan asked.

'Somewhere,' said Abu.

'But tell us where first,' I said.

Juan thought and then spoke. For me it was always the other way round. I was very impulsive but of course had regrets later – today was no exception.

'I'm coming,' was all I remember saying, but Nanny Ma did ask if I was sure, as it was going to be a very long day. I instantly thought, well, of course it's going to be a long day; we're going to England and I'm going first with Abu.

We walked hand in hand through the bazaar. My face had a big grin on it as I felt really special that day. Soon the sun had shown its full glory and my slim legs were tired. I asked my abu to carry me, but he kept saying, 'Just walk a little further.'

By the time he realised that I had stopped, there was a great distance between us. He insisted that I came forward to him to be picked up but I remained adamant that he come back to pick me up. After some short negotiations, he came back. The rest became an unbelievable nightmare. All I felt was a hot hand pressing down, and it was as if I had been thrown onto the heat of the land.

I awoke to realise that the heat on my back was from the harsh slap he gave me. And because of my weight, he had thrown me up over his shoulder to make the burden he was carrying lighter; his shoulder was also hot. I couldn't remember being hit, but the tears left scars on my emotions, probably for ever. Was my request unreasonable, or was I a burden, just a burden?

All I remember is that we were at a stranger's house. Everyone, including Abu, was happy – but not me. We ate, and by the evening we were in the van heading back home. When we were about to go to sleep, Juan asked me where we had been. I was so sad because I knew that this day had been an important day but I just didn't know why and how.

The smack had made me pass out, which hadn't helped. I didn't really hear very much. But something happened in that house that day that I was totally unaware of. The tears were throttling my throat and in reply to Juan's question I just said, 'I'm too tired.' I still held her hand over Nanny Ma, who always slept between us, as I slipped away into the land of the unknown.

Chapter Five

THE presence of the young female in our house had made my nanny ma and abu happy, but not us two. We were determined to find the unknown answers to our questions. We were so puzzled as to why she was in our house. What was her purpose? We didn't really want to know the answer. We were just happy to know that Nanny Ma, Abu and the both of us would be going to England that week.

Whoever she was, she had nothing to do with us. We always reassured each other about this and deep down inside we believed it.

She took over the household chores from Nanny Ma and both of the adults were very happy with her. Nanny Ma had less to do, therefore she spent some precious time with us two. Juan didn't really want to get close to the young woman at all and, as for me, I insisted on making life hell for her in a very short space of time. Whatever came into my head, I did. At meal times, I would often throw salt into the food when no one was looking, hoping that she would get told off; she didn't. Whilst eating, I would throw the food off my plate and make more work for her; she never complained. Even when my food was warm, I insisted that it was not hot enough. She would warm it again and again. She never got tired of work, or my pranks.

She had a lot of patience and perseverance, as when she was busy bathing, I would go into her room and tear her clothes. She knew it was me, but never complained to my father. Instead, she just said, 'Oh dear, this has a tear in it. Never mind.'

Hoping that she would get annoyed, I would ask, 'How come your clothes keep tearing? Well, answer! Ours don't.'

In reply, she'd say, 'I don't know, child.'

I would snap with anger, and leave.

Once, my nanny ma made tea, and I insisted that I take it to the woman, even though she said she didn't want any. I took the tea and, as I came towards her, slowly spilt it on to her lap. She looked down at her lap and started to wipe it with her scarf. She looked at me and said, 'It's fine. Don't worry.'

'Was it hot?' I asked quickly, hoping for a 'Yes.'

'Yes, it was, Kaashi. But never mind, child. You didn't do it on purpose.'

Maybe this perseverance was going to be her strongest point for her future with us.

The three of us dressed smartly, which meant no flip-flops, but sandals, except for Nanny Ma. She was old, that was why. She looked disillusioned and the tears that she was keeping back were making her eyes swollen. She carried us, one in each arm, and made us sit in the van. Abu sat in the front and we both moved to the sides, leaving space in the middle for Nanny Ma. The van moved off!

We looked back. The van had no back, so we could still see her. She was standing still but the tears were flowing so fast. She started to walk towards the moving van but we got further and further away. Her crying voice was drowned out by our loud screams of horror and betrayal as we both held hands and shouted, 'Nanny Ma, don't leave us!'

This agony lingered on in our hearts. It was even worse as we felt guilty because we had left *her*, not the other way round. The fourth person with us wasn't to be her but the new female we later knew as our stepmother. We felt betrayed, and feelings of poisonous hatred towards her became deep-seated in us. To some extent, Juan was never ready to rid herself of this hatred, even though our stepmother tried to get on. The hatred remained strong for ever, deep down in Juan's heart.

I still remember that day, so clear and yet clouded over with so many tears for so long.

Chapter Six

MEMORIES of our past life were quickly washed away as a new 'look' was forced upon us. Our long black curls were chopped off so we would fit into our new way of life. We got off the chairs to pick up the hair to keep, when suddenly the witch's broom swept it quickly away. In only a split second, it disappeared. Big men with big drums that shone so brightly took photos. My sister and I still remember that remarkable day with a copy of a photo, still hanging up, where we look so sad.

Years have gone by, in fact over forty, and yet those girls still look sad; their faces betray their hidden grief.

We became accustomed to the new life and new friends in a new environment. The friends helped us to settle into school and learn a foreign language. One particular friend shone in both our eyes; we both shared the same passion for him, which was almost destined. Whomever Juan liked, I did too. It was almost as if the two ugly sisters from *Cinderella* had a real prince to share, who guarded and protected them like a knight in shining armour.

His name was Martin, and, boy, did he look like a prince! His gorgeous looks, golden hair and good manners were enough for any eight-year-old to be besotted by. Looking back on it now, it really was almost like a scene from *Cinderella*; although ugly we were not, just jealous, infatuated with a boy whom no one else looked at. All the more for us! His infatuation with us both wasn't because of our good looks but our striking difference from the rest of the girls at school. They were all white and we were the only Asian girls.

We were infatuated with him for the same reason: we had never had white boys as friends before. He always asked, 'How come you're both different?' We were proud to be different then, but now it isn't seen as something positive.

He would come to our house every morning to walk us to school and at the end of the day he would wait to walk us home again. The days when Martin didn't come, we were always late for school. The day after this happened, Juan would give him the silent treatment but I would have a big grin on my face. That day I would get to hold his hand without his other hand being held by someone else. I had him all to myself. How joyful that experience was for me! It was as if I was falling in love with him each time, all over again.

That day his attention was on me only, his hand in mine, and Juan... well, she walked beside us. This fantasy never lasted as the next day everything was back to normal. Many times Juan and I would compare Martin to the boys back home. But there was no comparison. Martin was in our hearts and the others were in our minds. At our age, the heart ruled every time. How wonderful it felt to be loved by someone.

Chapter Seven

SIX new babies arrived in our family during the first six years of this life. Though we had no love or feelings at all for our stepmother we did adore the new additions, who we called the half-dozen. We felt responsible for them and as they grew so did our love for them. Their mother, our auntie as we called her, for we knew that she wasn't our real mother, was very affectionate towards her own six, but she had no affection for us. We needed a mother's love but never got any.

'Auntie Marian,' I called out one day. To my horror, she remained silent. I wanted to see her anger, as I had never seen it up to now. We weren't really allowed to call anyone who was much older than us by name. My father tried to look serious, but his eyes were smiling. He told me never to call out anyone's name – it was disrespectful.

When my father was at work, I would call her by her full name, Marian Bibi, and when she looked round I would change it to Auntie Marian. She didn't show any emotion – no anger, no happiness, no reaction. My teasing never angered her, but Juan's silence did have more of an impact on both of them. Deep down inside I was hurting because she had taken my mother's role but gave no motherly love to me or to my sister. I felt that she just didn't have love to give until I saw her with her own children. How wrong I was!

Juan and I would hear laughter and talking going on and would always leave our room quietly so as not to disturb anyone, and make our way to her bedroom. She would be in the middle of the bed with her half-dozen children gathered around her, all playing together. We two just looked on at what was rightfully ours but what we never got: playing, talking and sharing of motherly love. She kept kissing them and laughing. We both stood holding hands, barefoot, just inside the half-open door.

She would say, 'Come in.' But we wouldn't go in because we knew she didn't really want us to. We would look at each other, wipe each other's tears and go back to our room. We only played with the little ones when she was busy, not when she was there. At times like those, we would get on our bed, look out of the window and wait for our abu. As soon as he got out of his car, we made sure we were standing at the front door so we would be seen first. We were delighted because we would get picked up and kissed and cuddled, which made the whole day worthwhile again.

This particular day was just as ordinary as any other day and as our father sat down to have his tea after our family evening meal which Auntie always made, we were asked to come downstairs. On the way down, we told each other that we hadn't done anything terrible that day. I hadn't even done anything too disastrous at school.

'You haven't been telling on me again, have you?' I asked Juan.

'I thought you said you hadn't done anything today?' she replied smartly.

'Shut up and come down!' came the voice.

We sat almost as if we'd been summoned, and waited for our briefing. But this wasn't an ordinary briefing. My cousin, Solomon, was looking at us, my father was sipping tea and Auntie was just looking around the room.

'Tell them, Solomon,' said my father.

'Well... well, right. Er... Well, girls.'

'Oh, just tell them, Solomon. Get on with it.'

'Oh, Uncle Khan... Your nanny ma's dead,' he blurted out.

Silence.

'Girls, didn't you hear? Nanny Ma Sophia's dead.'

'Girls, girls!'

'You are lying. Nanny Ma can't die!' I shouted so loudly that everyone started to stare at me. In a reassuring way, my father asked me to calm down but I wasn't in the mood to be reassured. I looked at Juan who was sitting silently with both her hands clasped together between her legs. She was still staring at my cousin.

'Why are you telling me to calm down? We love Nanny Ma and she's the only one who loves us both so she cannot die, ever.'

My anger and Juan's silence had left them somewhat surprised. No one uttered a word; not us, not them.

As we got into our beds that night, I said goodnight to Juan. She said the same in return and then I asked, 'It's not true, is it, Jay?'

A very soft 'No' came in reply.

The remainder of that week was like the rest of the weeks: no sorrow, just happiness. Friday night was full of entertainment as we lived in a corner house opposite a pub. There was a lot of nightlife to see. People were talking, laughing, drinking, swearing; men and women were doing adult things. This is what we knew – things we giggled about but never mentioned.

In fact, every Friday and Saturday night, we turned off our light so our parents would think we were asleep, but then we would open the window, lean out and just watch. It was almost as if we were at the pictures.

Early on Saturday morning, a few people started coming to the house. We thought nothing of it until we saw Solomon again. This time he wasn't nice. Instead he grabbed me by my arm so that I couldn't move, and asked, 'Where's the big one?'

'Inside,' was my reply.

He pulled me in and held my sister by the hand. He took us into the kitchen keeping a firm grip on me all the time. He sat down and looked at both of us. There was hurt and anger in his eyes as well as a look of frustration on his face. He shouted, 'She really is; you have to accept it! Oh God. She was, on that day when I told you, not today. Do you understand? She's gone to a better place – heaven!'

'You liar,' I blurted out.

Juan looked at me and then said quietly, 'He's not lying. It's true. Nanny Ma has gone to our mummy.'

I ran outside and went to the end of the road where children picked blackberries. I went through the broken fence and sat on the dirty ground amongst the prickly bushes, picking blackberries. I put them all in my lap. My dress was dampened by the juice of the berries but I didn't care as I sat separating the ripe berries from the unripe ones. I then counted the berries, ripe ones for me, unripe ones for Nanny Ma. I wanted more unripe berries so that just maybe things would brighten up when I got home but no, there were many more ripe ones. In our culture we believed that less berries meant fewer days of life; how true that was that day.

The tears were running down fast around the corners of my nose and streamed straight into my mouth. But they didn't change the taste of the fruit that I squashed into my mouth. My watery, blurred eyes could see only blackberries. Then there were no more to eat, but I had many more thoughts; I was hurt and confused and full of angry tears. Someone, please hear my tears of silence. Please hear me cry. Everyone is far away.

My loud cries became silent tears, no one to cry for, no one, no more!

Chapter Eight

IN our society, women stayed at home while men went out to work. Women cooked, cleaned and made sure that everything was exactly the way that *they* liked it upon their return from work. I emphasise the word 'they' because the male is the head of the family. He gets the most respect and therefore everyone, including his wife, calls him 'they' rather than him or by his name. This is almost how we now speak to royalty. However, in return, the husband always called the wife 'you' or called her by her name.

Women talked quite loudly when with other females, but with males, the woman was seen and not heard. What he said was usually the accepted decision. Most, but not all, wouldn't answer the father or husband back. They lived a life where this was the norm. In our household this was certainly true.

My sister and I would often try to push issues to our liking but normally we would know when to shut up. Our father would sometimes listen and accept what we were saying but at other times it was better not to be told, 'Shut it or else it will get shut.'

Auntie Marian, our stepmother, did exactly what she was told the first time by her husband and as I always told her, as well as others, she was far too soft for her own good. She certainly didn't like it but accepted it; she was told, like all females at the time of marriage, that they have the respect of their fathers and the only way to keep that respect is to make sure they please their husbands. The only time that you ever leave your husband is when you're being buried. She will certainly obey this rule until he dies.

It was a cold, damp winter's day when we both came home from school. The house seemed very quiet. The younger ones were sitting quietly rather than playing and making a lot of noise. My father was sitting in the sitting room, smoking. He had the television on, but he wasn't really watching it. Auntie Marian wasn't downstairs as normal.

My heart started to beat very fast and my body started to shake with fear, for I knew something wasn't right. I could hardly get the words out; feeling embarrassed, stuttering, I said hello to my father. I looked at him but he didn't look back. He just said, 'You're back.'

As I walked up the stairs, afraid to see what I didn't want to see, and wishing that it wasn't going to be true, I opened the door of the bedroom she shared with her children. I stood there gasping for breath, speechless at what I saw. She sat, silently sobbing; carefully, without hurting her bruised, blackened eye, she wiped away the tears so they couldn't be seen. Her lips were also red, as if some force had been applied. I dropped my school bag and moved my jelly-like body to go and sit on the floor between her legs. If I looked through the tears in my own eyes, it was almost as if the bruises were less severe, but as the tears fell from my eyes, the bruises became clear again.

'Why do you let that bastard do this to you?' I shouted angrily.

She just replied as she had done once before. 'What can I do? I am a woman. He is my husband.'

'You should hit him back, beat him when he's not looking or stab him when he's asleep.' Oh, God help her. 'Why don't you just leave him, the bastard?'

'I can't do that. He's my husband and where would I go? I have no relatives in this country and anyway, it will only be my corpse that will leave him one day—'

I started blurting out something even though she was still talking. 'That's why he does this to you. Why can't you be strong like me? I can help you to escape and leave him. Then he'd know it. Do you want me to do something to him? I will even say that it was my idea. By God, I will kill him one day.'

Naturally she said no, and told me to be calm. I felt sickened at the truth; it had been a nightmare before and now it was happening again. I lay my head on her lap and felt her tears running down my forehead to merge into my tears, which together streamed off my nose and onto her thighs. I cannot remember how long I lay there but suddenly I heard footsteps coming up the stairs.

I got up, shut her door behind me and went into my room. I put the bin into my lap to be sick into but nothing came out. I put my face on the pillow. That evening was different as there was the echo of the day's tragedy.

My father was cooking in the kitchen. As Auntie didn't come down I took her food up to her and then I sat with the young ones to eat with them.

He had taken his food into the sitting room. Juan didn't come down for dinner either. No one talked about it. If she could accept it, why couldn't I? Was I too independent? Or was it the fact that embedded deep down inside me were feelings of shame and hatred as if poison had been injected into my body, and every time that something happened that poison ran through my blood all over again.

Slowly but surely it was killing the child inside of me, snatching away my childhood and making me a woman before I was old enough to be one.

Chapter Nine

It was my first day at secondary school and I still remember that it was on that day my father manipulated me into sleeping in his room on the spare bed for the very first time. I had refused but then he *told* me – he didn't ask me. I was too naïve and I listened to him. It was so unbearable that it was hard for me to forgive or to forget and even more so to live with. It was like a nightmare that kept repeating itself every so often.

This gave me the tools to hate him for ever into old age and even though it stopped a long time ago, the feelings embedded inside me have marked my body and mind. Now I don't see him any more because he lives so far away. This means that the tears of silence don't run as often.

He asked me to come into his bed because he was cold. The next couple of minutes were to be the most horrifying ordeal for me. He put his hands over my mouth and his body on top of mine, and this horrible, slimy person looked at me, almost like a monster. He satisfied his own pleasures, which he should have been doing with his wife. On many occasions I said no, but he was always able to find me at home on my own at some point.

I remained his property until I became someone else's; the 'someone else' was my husband. Even though I was strong and independent, the shame I felt and the honour of the family meant that I could share the nightmare with no one. Good, decent, respectable people keep each other's self-respect intact. Who would believe a child and, if he found out, what would he do and where would I go?

Auntie Marian was a simpleton and either didn't know what was happening, or didn't want to know. After all, what could she have done anyway? The only one who could understand was someone who was experiencing it herself. I just accidentally happened to witness such a person's torture with my own eyes.

We had an uncle who was well respected; we all used to go to him for advice because he was one of the oldest members of the family. Uncle Daaniaal lived in a house he had bought; this was rare, as everyone else rented places and lodged together. He lived with his family of six girls and one son, Sohail. His wife, Rose, had passed away and he remained devoted to her; he vowed to keep her name alive by never remarrying and bringing up the seven children himself.

The six girls took over the running of the family house and were very proper and domesticated. All of them were very confident and assertive except one, the youngest, Dinaag. She was passive and lacked all the skills that the others had because she had been the closest to her mother and had been at a young age when her mother had died.

Everyone loved and spoilt the son because he was the only son; this meant that his word was law. He dominated and suppressed those he could, and, as he was the eldest of the children, he ruled the ones who allowed it.

It was a midsummer day and I had bunked off school to go to the pictures. I got there late and the show had started. I couldn't go back because I might have been caught, as I had been before. So why not make the best of the day? I caught a bus and went to Dinaag's house as I knew that no one apart from the girls would be at home during the day. I knocked on the front door.

There was no reply, no noise, nothing. I went round the back and opened the kitchen door. I then knew that someone was in, as the kitchen door was always unlocked if someone was there. I went in, calling, 'Hello. Hello. Anyone home?'

There was silence, but then came the faint sounds of crying. The noise was near, but still faint. It seemed to be coming from the bathroom at the end of the kitchen. I knocked on the door and the noise stopped. I could hear breathing. 'Dinaag, are you inside?'

I didn't even know why I called her name. I certainly didn't know who was inside, but I had a gut feeling. On the other hand I didn't expect the scene that met my eyes. The door swung open and Sohail came out in a fury, his head down. I didn't really look at him as he brushed past me but I did see Dinaag. She lay on the floor, naked; her long waist-length wet hair plastered around her covered some of the shame she felt.

Her body was trembling and the floor was wet; I could tell that either she had been dragged out of the bath or she had got out in a hurry. I went up to her and handed her the towels from the floor. She didn't look up at me but instead she wrapped herself up in the towels and just said, 'I'm fine. Go and make yourself some tea while I get ready!'

Get ready! Can anyone ever be ready for this, or ready for anything after this? Was I?

Chapter Ten

My feelings of hatred weren't just in my heart but flowed outside it just as when someone tells you they have cancer and it has spread through to other parts of the body. There comes a time when they're at the final stages of life and there's already been a knock at death's door. They're just waiting for whoever is there to open it. In our case and in many other cases too, I'm sure, it isn't the bitter physical end of life but this bitter-sweet death endured every so often. It's something you feel you cannot control, and, though you don't want to accept it, you hope no one will know, so you live alone with this secret.

The anger makes it bitter and it's sweet because you cannot tell anyone how awful it is, so you fake a smile. It's like death because it feels like the end of the world. Can you ever imagine ever coming close to death but then having to face it again and again? We cannot force this end as, in our religion, it's a sin to end one's life.

If I had not witnessed the horrifying scene as if it were from a movie, I would never have known, but now Dinaag could never hide it from me. I never told her about my ordeal, but at least when I broached the subject she didn't deny hers. It was almost like a consolation to know that someone else was experiencing the same as me. I never really knew if she guessed or not, for she never mentioned it. But to lighten my ordeal, I would mention hers to make my pain a little easier to bear. It was almost like taking a painkiller, which numbs your senses for a very short while. That night was a night of a thousand deaths; it made me feel hopeless, frightened and very fragile.

Although Dinaag never really wanted to talk about her ordeal, I always encouraged her to do so, even though I could tell she wasn't happy about going over it again and again, but somehow it eased my pain. It wasn't because *I* talked about it but because she described a lot of what I was feeling. I often told her to tell her father or sisters, and that is what I wanted to do, but who would believe me? Would everyone get to know? Would people look down on me?

'Oh, there's that girl who has accused her father of all sorts of shameful things.' 'Dirty, oh how dirty.' 'This is how children repay their parents! Tut, tut!'

Maybe I could live with that, as I was thick-skinned in more ways than one, but my father wouldn't accept it. Everyone near and far wouldn't accept what I said. The one thing that I remember Dinaag telling me – that stuck in my brain and heart – was that if people knew, there was no way that most males would ask for your hand in marriage. After all who would want a disgraced girl? The only hope would be to marry someone much older or divorced, or someone with a string of children left behind by his dead wife.

After all, most men always say, 'an experienced girlfriend but a virgin wife'. This belief is embedded into a lot of our people's brains. For example, my cousin, Hashi Bi, at the mere age of nineteen, had to be married off to fifty-nine-year-old Suba Karim. She had been engaged to be married to her cousin Yakood, who, later on, changed his mind as he went off to America to work and study. The engagement broke and the first person to ask for her hand in marriage was accepted by her parents, even though it was not her own fault that it had been broken off. Her parents had a long period of mourning and this ended when Suba Karim's offer came. After all, they counted themselves lucky, as his children were all married and gone. They married within a few weeks, and she settled in with his extended family. If we have embraced a culture like this, then what hope do we have?

She was seen as a reject, punished by our society and rewarded by a man. Yes, a man, who did her a big favour by marrying her.

If my secret were told, what would my punishment be? Would I also want a man to favour me and taunt me for every day of my life, calling me filthy, dirty and unwanted. No soap in the kingdom could wash away a dirty sin like Hashi Bi's, according to the locals, so what realistic chances did I have to bare all?

Above all, I did not want to be married off at the tender age of twelve to a man who could have been older than my father.

I knew my secret had to live and die with me alone.

Chapter Eleven

MALE domination is prevalent in our households – men are regarded as superior. The man makes the household rules most of the time and women accept them. The most they can do to show and to feel that they have power is to take control of domestic issues and issues involving the children. This was the only power they could claim to be theirs. In our house, total power remained with our father. I often wonder how different my life could have been if my stepmother had taken control.

I fantasised that if my own mother had been alive, I would never have had male domination thrust upon me. I think I could have hoped for a better life, one we all crave for. It's quite sick to think that being raped by a close family member is nothing compared to being raped by an outsider. We often hear of how someone in the village did this to so and so and how the family tried to bring charges against him. But people are paid off and the victim is left to take a small sum of money for the inconvenience caused.

What price would they put on the emotional torture that the woman faced? But being a woman means that that isn't even a valid point open to discussion, even by the richest and most powerful men in that village. From the point of view of Western society he may not have more than a few thousand pounds, but his power, which is pure force and aggression, is exercised through his brothers or sons. The more money you have the more status you have.

The women in their households are usually better off and to a certain degree, have a better education than women in the rest of the society. They're respected and my God, do they know it as well! A lot of them can relate to current issues; they're aware of the oppression women live under and can indeed share their view, as long as it's only behind their own closed doors. Once they're outside, they never air their views.

A distant auntie, Zara, who was attacked herself as a young twelve-year-old, was made to feel that she was to blame for the sexual attack because she wasn't covered from head to toe, as some men would like women to be. This is brought to public attention when something goes wrong. Many, including family members, said that the only things that were showing were her face, hands and feet. In reply, the offender's female family members said that she had used her bewitching eyes to lure their son into doing things that he wasn't normally capable of, or would even think of. Daanish and his family members had only preached this for everyone else, as they all knew what kind of a boy he really was.

That was resolved very quickly by her staying silent; even now, thirty years on, she still talks to men with her head down; she never looks at them straight in the eyes as she does women. She has developed a very humble, quiet, almost passive personality and speaks only when spoken to, and laughs only in the presence of females.

Daanish has certainly left his manly mark on Zara, but she continues to live. Surely we were worse off than she was, but then I remember what her father, Abdullah, said: 'Oh child, for goodness sake, in the name of the almighty Allah, seal your mouth and never open it to hurl out words that will dishonour and bring disrespect to your father. I beg you with the attire on my head or else you'll see my dead face.' The 'attire' was a big piece of cloth that men who had respect wore on their heads, almost like a turban.

Once the man stopped wearing it in public it gave everyone ammunition to gossip and back bite. A father would hold his head up high but once something shameful happened, he would keep his head down in public places for quite a while. This was almost like a punishment for him, because daughters represented their father's honour.

Zara, unfortunately, became pregnant by Daanish, and the family spent days crying inside their home, not going out to show their faces in shame. It wasn't until the eldest member of the family, the great grandmother, decided that enough was enough and by crying all day, nothing would be resolved. She ordered a back street abortion to be carried out by the local midwife, who naturally had no qualifications, but had enough experience to know how to get rid of the foetus. This took place the same day, and the unborn was buried within the grounds of the house. She also spread the word that Zara was now ready for marriage, as she had not done anything wrong and was entitled to make a fresh start. A strong, determined woman – very rare, but possible.

Sufi, a forty-eight-year-old retired corporal, married her, much to her parents' delight, although he had lost his leg in the war. All ended well for Zara's parents, but maybe not for Zara. She had committed no crime – so why didn't she have a choice? I suppose it was better than being beaten up by her mother and her brother, Saif Ali, in the hope that she would die and rid them of the shame. She often said that she was shocked at how Ruhi, her own mother, a female like herself, could not understand the issue but could beat her so easily just because she could not bear to look at her because she no longer was a virgin. How could she wish her dead – the daughter she breastfed for two years? Unbelievable!

Domestic violence she could take, but verbal abuse was so hurtful. 'The dirt you're carrying in your tummy will curse you, us and your future family. The burden will not let you live; it will turn against you. You will be the mother of a bastard and bastards are never your own.' Unbelievable words of frustration from your own flesh and blood, truly unbelievable.

Chapter Twelve

I HAD never seen my mother and father together. Would he have been nasty and domineering towards her as well? Would she have put up with it? Thinking about it realistically, no one really knows. My stepmother was almost like a puppet in my father's hands. Her life was just a mere existence; she trod only in his footsteps.

Her mind was so easily influenced and, even though she knew what was right and wrong, she couldn't express her opinion in front of him. Behind his back her thoughts were quite logical really, but what a shame she never plucked up courage to defend herself or us. If she uttered a word that he disliked, he would just say, '*Quiet*!' and she would fall silent.

I remember the night when Father had been out drinking with his friends and came home really late, which was very rare. Though we all would pray that he stayed out for a long time, it never happened often enough. Drinking is a sin in our culture, even though many men even in those days were influenced by sheer indulgence and would secretly go off to the pub while denying ever going near the place. Some, including my father, had a bottle tucked away. He had his at the side of the armchair, which only he was allowed to sit on. If anyone dared to sit on it, like me, they would have to get up as soon as he entered the room. I confronted him about his bottle as only I dared; he maintained that he didn't drink from it often. It was just there for a very cold day and, of course, for medicinal purposes only.

'Yeah, right,' used to be my reply. Drinking, clubbing, womanising and gambling are all illegal for us. Women, though allowed to smoke in our society, are certainly not allowed to indulge in the rest. He always regularly reminded us of this and told us how good we were because we didn't indulge, but he never discussed himself. Why was he allowed? We all know these habits of self-indulgence can often get people into more trouble than they can handle and on many occasions, we, his family, had to handle and tolerate him.

That particular night has stuck in my mind. It was very late when I was woken from a bad dream – but the aftermath was worse than the dream itself. We were all fast asleep; children, as we know, are heavy sleepers and we didn't hear anything to start with. I do know that everyone except my father was at home. It was Juan who rudely woke me up by thumping me on the arm really hard and pulling my duvet right off. 'You stupid cow!' was what came out of my mouth, with my eyes only half open.

She looked very frightened and said, 'Oh shut up. Just get up and listen!'

I sat up and my eyes grew wide with fear at what I heard. We both rushed out of our room with nothing on but our very short nighties. We saw the most horrifying ordeal ever and the worst thing for any child to see. He was standing just inside the front door, pummelling her with his fists. She, our stepmother, had her arms over her face, trying to protect herself. She didn't retaliate in any way.

Apart from her crying, all we could hear was *thump*, *thump*. We ran down the stairs, our tiny bodies shaking, and tried to pull them apart. Juan kept pulling at them but he told her to go back upstairs. I was terrified but also so angry because I knew our pulling and Juan's pleading were doing no good at all. She kept saying, 'Stop it, Dad. Stop it, Dad…' How those words reverberated in my mind for so long.

Through frustration, I punched him in his private parts with my fist, just between his legs. Boy, did I punch hard! My fist was hurting. He pushed me out of the way, calling me a bastard and I shouted back at him, 'You are!' He pushed Marian up the stairs and trod on Juan.

I then grabbed his leg, but he kicked out with it to get it free and in the process made contact with my face. I remember the kick because his smart, polished shoes were so hard that my cheek was red for a few days. Everyone teased me at school, saying that I had been in a fight with someone, as I had been before. But no one knew the truth and I didn't tell them. My bruise was sore and would have bothered me a lot but in comparison to what I saw the following morning, it was nothing. Marian's whole face was blue, especially round the eyes.

I still remember his words – he said she deliberately didn't open the door because she was jealous because he had gone out and she didn't. He even accused her of locking the door from the inside so he couldn't come in because he was late. She was a simpleton and could have locked it by accident. I did ask her and she denied it; I believed her. She also said that she didn't hear him knocking at first, but when she did, she opened the door. He wasn't in the habit of listening but made sure that *he* was heard, if not willingly, then by force.

From that day on, for quite a while no one spoke to him properly. Marian carried on as normal and, thank goodness, not many people came to our house that week. If asked, quickly, like a good, faithful wife, she told people she had banged into the door. No one believed her or questioned her because they were embarrassed. As the bruises faded, so did her memory of the event, and she became quite normal again. Juan and I were still very upset, even though he had warned us to 'lose the attitude' or things would go badly for us. I just rolled my eyes; Juan just looked down and remained silent.

But as time passed, so did this incident. Even now, when I see Aunty Marian and my father, the very respectable Shoaib Khan, playing the role of the happy couple, it brings tears to my eyes to know how much she endured to stay married to him. Has it been worth it? Was it worth the miscarriage of the baby she named Diya, who she never got to hold in her arms because he kicked her in the stomach? So much truth, so hard to unravel. So many secrets, so many lies from Shoaib, and so many tears from Marian.

Is this how life is supposed to be?

Chapter Thirteen

My hatred for my father grew more and more, even though it wasn't really my battle all of the time. His domination of and superiority over us females, especially his wife, who was supposed to be on a level with him, made me hate him so much; it was a feeling I couldn't shake off. Christmas Eve was upon us again and, even though I had never declared that I also drank, somewhere deep down inside, everyone at home knew that I did. Sometimes the subject came up in conversation, and instead of lying and denying it, I just stayed quiet. I didn't want to lie so I stayed silent, often smiling, leaving everyone to make up their own minds.

I had always had a drink now and again, especially when there was a bottle behind his chair, but this Christmas Eve, I just didn't care. At the Christmas party hosted by my employers, I had a few drinks too many. I wasn't used to real heavy drinking so a few glasses taken down really quickly were more than enough. Everyone knew that I was a bit drunk so a colleague suggested I came to her flat and sleep it off. I did, as I was hardly fit to walk home. I was laughing and giggling and couldn't even walk straight. I wanted to go home and confront him but was in no state to do so.

After sleeping for a few hours, I awoke and decided it really was time to go home. I got home and went to my room. I was lying in my bed trying to recover. In the background I could hear my father asking Juan where I was. She muttered something quietly. Then I heard him shout out my name; I ignored him.

Then he shouted again, 'Little one, where the bloody hell are you!' this time really loudly. My youngest brother came in and told me that Dad was calling me. He talked for quite a while and then left saying, 'You'd better go, sis.' I got up and went.

My father told me to start tiling the bathroom, which he was trying to do. I did, but somehow I only managed to put one tile on the wall, as I couldn't focus on the task. My head was still fuzzy. He stood over me, watching my every move. He then started to growl words like, 'She thinks I don't know what she's been up to. She thinks I'm stupid, I know. Just look at her. Marian, come here and look at her. Juan, where are you? Come and see your sister.'

They both came up and he asked me why I couldn't tile the bathroom as I normally would have done. No one uttered a word. I stopped what I was doing, or rather stopped what I was unable to do. I looked straight into his eyes, those piercing blue eyes staring at me in anger. I wasn't sober enough to give the same stare back so I stood calmly looking right into his eyes.

He lifted his hand as he came close to hit me. I was concentrating so much that I didn't miss his action. I grabbed his hand. It wasn't hard for an eighteen-year-old to restrain a man of fifty. Staring at his hand for a while rekindled the torture of those fine lines. I threw his hand down; there was silence. Juan was gasping for breath.

He raised his hand again. Marian said gently, 'Leave her alone.'

Juan quickly stuttered, 'Please, Dad, she's a silly cow. Let her be!'

'Let her be? Let her be? She's drunk! Let her be?'

I turned around to get away, when suddenly he grabbed my arm forcefully. I tried to break free from him but I couldn't. Instead of pulling away from him, I pushed myself in his direction; he was near the wall. He was taken by surprise as I quickly put my hands around his neck.

His face and eyes showed no remorse, just disgust at what I'd done. But my eyes showed fury and my face was red, and since I was a very light-coloured child, it was obvious to see.

'You want to kill your father. Your father! Go on, little one.'

'I want you dead, and by God, one day you will be, if you carry on like this.'

'You've been—'

I cut him short. Louder than ever, I shouted, 'Yes, yes, I'm drunk. I've been drinking a few times but you do it most of the time. You go to the casino and lose all our money, including mine. And then you come home and beat Auntie. My God, you're a devil in a human's body. You'll get what's coming to you, real quick.' I shook my head in disgust a few times at him, as if the roles had reversed.

With that, I rushed into the bathroom again to be sick. I pretended to be sick for a long time, all the while listening out for the drama outside. But there wasn't one. It was all very quiet. I opened the door and there was no one there.

I went into my room. Juan had her disapproving look on her face yet again. I looked at her, raising my eyebrows. Then I got back into bed. I really don't remember the rest of the evening but I'm sure I slept throughout.

Chapter Fourteen

I STILL remember how I felt when I was in love with a dashing, gorgeous, sexy looking boy in our school. He was the only one I had ever loved after Martin. Martin was my love in the infant years as Iqbal was my love in my teenage years. I knew I loved Iqbal but he loved anyone who looked at him. I was besotted with him – you could call it love or infatuation.

Where he went, I wanted to go. Where he sat, I wanted to sit. He flirted with anyone who wanted to be flirted with; I was just one of many. He always walked with the wind blowing his hair and his tie. I wasn't the only one he let down, as Juan was also a hot contender fighting for his attention. Why was it that out of the whole school, he was the only one for both of us?

I would often flirt with other boys in the hope of making him jealous but no such luck. There were many times that I, as a girl, would fight with a boy and then talk to Iqbal to get sympathy, hoping that we would share some time together. Even that didn't work as planned. In spite of everything, I still felt the same for him. On many occasions I would think, Why is it I don't feel that way for my husband-to-be, Sahel? I felt more for my distant uncle, Shahid, whom, yes, we both loved very much but he, a womaniser, had loved us both for different reasons.

Neither of us could ever confront each other's feelings for Iqbal or Shahid. Juan, sensible and sensitive; me, well, feminine on the outside, tomboy on the inside, assertive and unpredictable. Neither of us got them anyway.

I didn't have any feelings for the man I was to get – Sahel.

I never wanted to marry or, if I did, it was to be either for love or money. He had money but not as much as six zeroes – that's what I call money – a million. He was educated, had enough money, and a comfortable lifestyle, which he wanted to mould me into. He was born in Britain and therefore was very westernised. Or at least that was the impression that most people got.

On numerous occasions I questioned myself: Why am I marrying him? After all, it was my choice. Why did I say yes, when I meant no? Somehow I just knew deep down inside that he wasn't right for me. I needed someone who would let me be free, let me be myself. I think it was just the excitement of marriage.

And you know what they say – the grass is always greener on the other side. I wanted to take that chance of being loved by someone even if I never loved him. After all, I never got anyone I loved. At the age of eighteen, should I have known better? I should have known not to play with fire – we all know that. Maybe not every time but at least sometimes you could get burnt.

Many people had promised me that they loved me more than their own life, and marriage was the way to go but I hadn't felt the same way. That didn't stop me from letting them say how they felt, but nothing more. After all, flattery was good for my confidence and therefore I never stopped them saying what they wanted to say.

My father knew I was too young to be married yet and ideally he wouldn't have wanted me to. He just wanted to tame this rebel and that was the respectable way to do it.

The winter's gloom and doom had a silver lining. I knew that once winter ended spring would be taken up with preparations, and summer – well – that would be very quickly gone. As soon as spring came there were new buds on the trees, colours changed and the warmth of the sun created beautiful blossoms. My hibernation would also end:

after being tame for a few months I was back to my old self again. Somehow the spring and summer just have that happy feel to them.

I had just come home from work, and I still remember everyone, including the six younger children, all sitting watching *Top of the Pops* on BBC television. Everyone was just concentrating on the television. I slowly looked at each and every one of the nine but no one looked at me. I just quietly said, 'Hi, half-dozen.'

'Hi, sis.'

'I've made a decision.'

'Yes, we know. You want to be a big doctor, sis.'

'No.'

'No? OK. You don't want to be a doctor, sis. Fine.'

'Yes.'

'Make your mind up, sis!'

'Dad, I'm talking to you.'

'That's fine, child. You don't have to be anything you don't want to be. Once you're married, you can do whatever you want.'

'Once I'm married is the problem. I don't want to get married!' I closed my eyes, afraid of the reply and quickly got up and left the room.

As I climbed the stairs I could no longer hear the TV or any voices at all. I waited just inside my bedroom, with the door wide open. I listened out for any response. Slowly, one by one, everyone left the sitting room, except one. I went downstairs into the kitchen where Juan and Auntie were busy making tea. Juan looked at me out the corner of her eye. I took some food and went back up. Then Juan came up and kept giving me disapproving looks without saying anything.

Auntie didn't come up. I stood at the top of the stairs trying to listen to her conversation with my father. I couldn't hear anything.

Chapter Fifteen

A COUPLE of months had gone by. No one talked about my marriage and in return I didn't mention it either. I assumed that it was all clear. I did, however, know that the three adults discussed it whenever possible and every time I came into the room, they went quiet. I wanted to know what they were all saying but at the same time was glad that no one mentioned it to me. During that period, even Sahel didn't phone me or come round to see us while I was at home. No one even mentioned Sahel or his family.

Even though I was no longer getting married the wedding date stuck in my mind. It was a Sunday morning and the sun was shining brightly through the curtains. I opened my eyes and turned over to face my side table. Juan was still fast asleep as I could hear her snoring; she had her back to me. I slowly picked up my diary and opened the page: Sunday, 7 August. I turned a few more pages: Sunday, 14 August – 'My wedding day'.

I pulled the tiny pen out of the diary pocket and scribbled over the entry 'My Wedding Day'. Instead I wrote 'Pakistan Independence Day'. I put the diary back, turned over again, closed my eyes and went back to sleep. Despite the fact that the week was very busy at work and at college, I hadn't forgotten its significance.

My auntie and uncle arrived on Friday afternoon before I got home; it was a nice surprise to see them. I wasn't as surprised to see them as they were to see me! Why? We greeted each other with hugs and kisses as normal but rather than sitting around and doing nothing as guests normally do, they were busy. All the adults, about half a dozen, were in the sitting room with the door shut. I could hear people talking but couldn't make any sense of it.

Twice I went into the room, and each time they all became uneasy and stopped talking. I felt uneasy too and as everyone remained quiet, on both occasions I went out again. I stayed in the kitchen instead. I asked Zubi, the youngest, what everyone was doing. 'We don't really know, sis. Something's up.'

The eldest replied, 'We don't know as no one tells us, do they? They've been in that room all afternoon.'

Zubi then told me that he'd seen Mum and Auntie, along with big sis, going up to Mum's room. I asked them to go to the sitting room to find out what they were talking about. I suggested that the twins, Zia and Zen, go upstairs to see what was going on up there.

Instead, Rishab and Vinny both got up and went to leave the room. Rahul, the eldest, asked them to sit down for he knew that they were full of mischief as always and were probably going to head upstairs.

'What's the matter? Don't you want to help?'

'We do, sis. But we've already been in trouble once today because of Zia and Zen. You see, when we were in the sitting room, Dad and Auntie started talking about someone going somewhere. We were looking at them. They then asked us to go and play. After a short while we went back inside,' said Rahul.

'Dad started shouting, demanding even, that either we stay outside or go into the dining room. Zia and Zen were really scared, but you know, Rishab and Vinny, always glued together, had already quietly gone upstairs to go through everyone's bags; no one noticed they were missing. But now look, they're ready again. Zubi nearly got a slap because he said, "Why should we? We want to sit in this room." He was lucky that Uncle saved him, otherwise Dad's slap across his ears would have made them ring for a week like last time. You remember, sis, don't you?'

'Of course, yes. We had to put warm oil into his ear before he got better. Right. Never mind. Sit down. I know. Why don't you all watch a video? I'll come and watch it with you.'

I felt really stupid because I'd tried to use the boys and Zia, a quiet and gentle girl, to satisfy my curiosity. But I did have the right to know, as this definitely had something to do with me and I was the only one not involved with the half-dozen. I went into the sitting room!

'How come you've come today, Uncle? You didn't tell us you were coming.'

'Well, my love, I had the weekend off so your auntie suggested we come here.'

My auntie quickly came over to me and took my hand between her hands. 'Have we got to have a reason to come over, dear?'

'No, of course not. But what's all the "hush hush" for?'

'No, no, dear. Listen, there is nothing like that. No "hush hush" at all. Just some family problems, you know.'

'No, I don't know.'

'Oh child, please don't worry. Everything will be fine. Let's go upstairs and talk.'

As we sat on my bed she showed me her hand, fully painted with henna. She said that henna should always be worn by young girls. Female hands should never be bare. She insisted on putting a little on me. I said no but she replied that Friday was the best and holiest day of the week and in her childhood that was the day mama put henna on all the girls, including my mum. How could I refuse now?

Then she said, 'Please let me fulfil my wish, my child.'

She made a small intricate design on my hands and feet. It

made my hands and feet feel so cold that I lay flat on the bed with my duvet on top, waiting for the henna to dry.

The noise of people coming up and down the stairs, together with the distant voices of women, was enough to wake anyone up. I looked at the clock with only one eye half open. Too early to get up! Too much noise for eight o'clock. I turned over – no Juan! I tried really hard to stay asleep but couldn't because the question kept going round in my mind: Why is Juan up?

She wasn't an early riser. And never in my life had there been so much noise so early in the morning. So what was happening? I pulled the door handle to open the door. It was stuck! I pulled harder but it still wouldn't open.

I pulled and tugged. I looked at the lock: the door was locked from the outside. No one had ever locked the door before! I was almost in a state of frenzy and started to shout hysterically. 'Juan, Juan, open the door! Auntie, open the door! Dad, Dad! Rahul! Rishab! Vinny! Oh, anyone, please! Open the door! Oh, why isn't anyone opening the door?'

Everyone could hear me – I could hear *them* but no one was taking any notice of me. Why? Tears ran down my cheeks, clouding my vision. It was almost as if the monsoon rains were battering on a heated surface, creating a misty atmosphere. Had there been a thunder and lightning storm before I awoke? This barrier between me and the rest of the world was almost like the Berlin Wall. I couldn't see over it or through it.

As I sat leaning against the door my rolls of thunder reduced to tears of silence. But I wasn't alone. My ears could hear my own sobbing but my heart heard the sobbing of someone so young, yet so brave, to have taken the risk for me; tears must have been silently running down their face. I quietly asked who was outside. But no reply came in the form of words.

Instead the answer was given with different tones of breathing and sobbing. Silence means 'don't know'; sobbing is for bad news.

'Zia?' I asked… the sobbing got louder.

'Zen.' He stopped, silent, for a short while.

I put my own grief to one side as I realised that someone else was suffering for me. I knew that something bad was happening. The one person who was alone and not involved was me. Little did I know that I was to be in the centre of it all without even being aware.

'What are you doing here? Move.'

I heard the key turn in the lock.

I moved away from the door, otherwise it couldn't open. In came Juan and behind her, my ex-bridesmaid-to-be, Dhaani.

'Hurry up and get ready, Kaashi. Today's a special day for you. It's your day. Be ready soon.'

'What? I don't understand.'

She moved aside and in Dhaani's hands I could see a wedding dress with all the trimmings.

'I don't understand, Juan.'

'Oh, stop being childish and get ready.'

'Is it my funeral today?' I cried loudly.

'No. Your wedding,' came the sarcastic but true reply.

Well, how was I supposed to know? Did anyone tell me or give me a chance to find out?

Chapter Sixteen

WHEN I look back at my wedding day, even now I remember it very clearly: how my outfit was made without my knowing about it; how I was transformed into a bride. I said no but the priest was told yes. The ceremony was at the local village hall but surely it had been booked for the 14th August, not the 13th? Who changed it? Why was I not told that it had been changed?

Hadn't I said that I didn't want to get married anyway? As I left the family home for the first time in my life, my auntie started the farewell ceremony, reminding me that my new home was now my only home, a place where I would live and die.

As I silently cried on her shoulder, I whispered, 'How could you, Auntie Libby? I trusted you.' She looked at me as she kissed me, with a look of sympathy on her face.

Her last words were, 'I'm sorry, child. Be happy.'

Uncle Terry quickly came and put his hands over my head, saying, 'Bless you.'

If everyone else had deceived me, why had I had such high expectations of her? After all, she was only my own mother's sister. Who else was she? No one. At least no one to me, not now, anyway. Everyone had turned their back on me.

Everyone looked happy and said how beautiful the bride looked. No one could see my emotions. No one knew how I felt except my bridesmaid. It wasn't her fault. She was only carrying out orders. Our conversation that day was lengthy but the most daunting thing that I remember was that nothing had been cancelled!

They had simply changed the date: the venue was booked to the day before so it would be unexpected, just in case I rebelled. Hence the way my door had been locked so I couldn't escape the day. I remember the last thing I asked her, 'How long have you known, Dhaani?'

'Since last week. I was told it was to be a surprise,' she replied.

The journey to my new home was bearable as I was reconciled to the fact that this was my destiny – a hole that had been dug for me. The top surface was my parents' house; the hole was my married life and the bottom of the hole was death. Thinking of death, I climbed out of the car to new surroundings. This isn't where Sahel lives... or is it? I wondered.

I was taken straight upstairs to be greeted by the father-in-law; his giant figure overshadowed me. He offered me money for marrying his son. I didn't look up at all as it was customary to look down until all rituals had been performed. The fat, big-breasted woman who was breathing heavily like a heathen troll, chanted religious prayers, thanking God for giving her a young daughter-in-law who would bring new members into her household.

All I was aware of was her massive size, especially her lack of waist, and her stomach, which was level with my eyes. At times when she moved, my view was even obscured. Her distinctive smell left a more lasting impression. There was a bad odour every time she lifted or moved her arms. All I could think at that moment was, I wish I had my deodorant with me. I could pay for her blessings with this gift unknown to her.

After everyone had left the room, I was told to stay seated until the groom came. I did so. He took a long time coming and even though I had enough time to prepare myself, nothing in the world could have actually prepared me for him. When he came in, my veil was over my face. He turned off the light, locked the door and got into bed. He started to take his clothes off and demanded that I took mine off too. What a creep, I thought. I ignored him, instead starting to pull off my bangles.

He grabbed my arm and pulled me down. He started to pull off my dress. I shouted, 'Stop it, Sahel. What are you doing?'

'Oof, Allah. Don't repeat your boyfriend's name ever again otherwise you'll go straight to hell. Oh God, forgive her, she is a sinner, Allah! She is a devil in a woman's body.'

Although his grip was still tight on my arm, I could move it; it fell onto something that was so smooth. I was puzzled. What was it that I had just felt? I felt it again. I was right the first time. It was someone's head – his head. Had Sahel shaved his head? Had he turned religious or become a fashion guru?

I listened to his breathing as he put his heavy chest on me. How could Sahel be this flabby? I wasn't imagining any of this. I was feeling reality without seeing it. I searched for the light; I remembered the pull cord near the wall at the top of the bed. I pulled it and screamed with fear at the sight on top of me. Now it all made sense.

The person lying on the same bed as me was a middle-aged man, at least fifty years old. A fat, unattractive, bald man, with some side teeth missing, gawping at me, like a lion waiting for a feast. He quickly said, 'Now, listen. Don't show me up.'

'Who are you?'

'Oh, Allah. Tell her who I am. I have wasted so much money on marrying her and she asks who I am. Have you no shame, girl? Fear God first and me second.'

I couldn't believe what I had married. I didn't know; I hadn't seen him until then. I told him I would scream if he touched me. I turned to the wall and pretended to sleep. After only a few minutes I could hear a noise like thunder coming from his mouth. I could feel the after-effects of the noise – the wetness on my dress.

I had to bear it. I had nothing else to wear and nowhere to run. Where were my other clothes? I tried to sleep. When my arm ached from sleeping on it, I turned over and imagined what the sight in front of me was. How naïve had I been? Why had I trusted everybody?

As dawn broke I could clearly see his open mouth; he was coughing and spluttering at me. As he breathed out a sigh, his nostril hair moved up and down. He was the perfect giant we know from fairy tales. The odour from his mouth was almost as if the sewage canal had all of its barriers lifted. The spit it sprayed was enough to soak my face.

That night was a living nightmare. I didn't really sleep at all because I wasn't used to sleeping with anyone else, especially with noises throughout. He awoke, got up and told me to grow up and stop making a joke of myself. He told me to get downstairs quickly to my family. He unlocked the door, put the key back in his pocket and left.

I stood still at the living room door, in my wedding dress, looking almost as if I had not slept at all. The mother-in-law was chuckling loudly, but fell silent when she saw me. She hurriedly took me back upstairs and asked the maid to bring all my suitcases up and help me to get ready. Once we were in the bedroom, I told the maid to hang up my clothes. I got ready.

I went downstairs an hour later, still in a state of shock. The mother-in-law made me sit next to her at the breakfast table, asking me or rather telling me to eat more and more. The amount she put in front of me was enough for a whole household. I had tea but nothing to eat. As I drank my tea I looked around the table.

Who are these people? Who are they to my family? What is the connection between them and me? They were strangers. How had I managed to get married into a household that I'd never seen before? I was faced with question after question but there were no answers – none that I knew, anyway!

Chapter Seventeen

A WEEK had gone by in this strange new environment. No one from my family came to visit, which gave me plenty of time to build bridges with this new family. Everyone was very nice to me, especially the mother-in-law. I knew the reason why. She would always say to her guests that her son was lucky to get such a young and beautiful wife who would be able to give him and them the family they so desperately wanted. This was the only reason to get him married off and the only reason they needed me.

So to keep me there, they did whatever made me happy. There was no cooking, cleaning, washing, ironing or any other chore for me to do. So what could I do with the time? They had made it perfectly clear that no female in their family went out to work. So I was free to go out shopping, go to restaurants, the cinema and so on, with no questions asked, as long as I never used public transport. Everyone at home had access to a car or a driver if need be.

They were not rich but could easily afford cheap labour brought over from Pakistan in return for food and a place to live.

That one week gave me time to think and reflect on this new life. After all, I had lots of time and very little to do. Father and mother-in-law stayed at home. My husband, Mirza Hussein, and his three brothers all worked hard in their own import-export business. They left early and came back late.

There was no other daughter-in-law, as Mirza was the eldest and thus the first to marry. He had spent all his life building up the business and now it was time to settle down. They were, of course, searching for young wives for the other three men too. Looking at them together, anyone could see that the reason they had not married earlier was not the business; they were having too much fun after working hours to have ever missed out on anything. A wife was not something they had needed before; it was only because of their age it became a necessity, especially if they wanted the family name to continue.

At the end of that week, I was looking forward to going back to my parents' house – that was customary. Early Saturday morning when I went down for breakfast my mother-in-law told me that my mother and father had just phoned to say that they were coming before lunch to get me. She went on to say that we would all have lunch in the conservatory together as a big happy family. I replied, 'OK, Auntie Laila.'

She then reminded me as I was going upstairs after breakfast to make sure that I dolled myself up well like a bride. I rolled my eyes at her but she just smiled back. I think she knew that seven days of looking like a bride was a bit too much for me.

When the doorbell rang, Jacob, the house worker, opened it. It was my parents; he took their bags from them and placed them in the hallway. He asked everyone to go in and be seated. I waited at the top of the stairs, listening to them talking happily, chatting to one another. I didn't really feel like coming down.

How would I greet them? What would I say? I was so hurt that I didn't want to see them or talk to them.

'Come down, child,'

'Yes, Uncle.'

I had to go down now. So I did, and stood in the doorway. 'Oh my child. Come here. Take my blessings,' uttered my father. He quickly got up and as I came forward, he put his hand over my head, a sign of offering blessings. He was smiling; he looked really smug.

Auntie and Juan got up and both kissed me. They both looked at me without smiling because they knew they had deceived me. I looked at them and then looked away. Auntie Laila started abruptly: 'Come, child. Sit here with me. Oh Majnu, my sweetie, move over and make some room for our daughter.'

She always spoke to her husband in this way and he was very comfortable with it. My stepmother would never speak to her husband like that; but why? I sat next to her and all I could say was, 'How are the half-dozen, I mean, the little ones?'

Their mother speedily replied, 'They're all well and looking forward to seeing you.'

We were all silent in the car on the way to my parent's house, but as I went through the front door, I had so many questions about that day a week before. The little ones all came running up to me, hugging me, smiling, kissing me and talking. They pulled me over to where they were sitting, and talked for the rest of the evening. When they went off to bed, so did I.

My room was exactly the same. I sat on my bed alone and cried. I cried for so long that I dozed off without realising it. I remember how I sobbed. My eyes were so swollen and puffy I could hardly see.

I awoke to find myself in yesterday's clothes. Once again I turned over and grabbed my diary – Sunday, 14 August. There were the words: 'Pakistan Independence Day'. I added 'Good' and then for Saturday, 13 August, I put 'My Wedding Day – bad'. No one had turned the pages over so I did that day.

Sunday, 21 August. Slowly I wrote 'Last day in this house. Goodbye diary.'

A little later I sat beside my father but he pretended not to acknowledge that I was there. I blurted out my question: 'Why, Dad? Why did you do this?'

Auntie and Juan left the room. He looked at me with love, but also with guilt. He explained how he thought he would lose his honour if he didn't get me married off. Because I had said no to Sahel, he had said yes to these people, because they were very respectable. Parents can arrange their children's marriages.

The only reason he hadn't told me was because he'd thought that I wouldn't be happy. I might have run away to escape the marriage. He explained that he couldn't afford to have respect for him go down the drain. The way that I had made the decision had made him feel he couldn't control me so he had taken charge and controlled the situation the best way he could. After all if I lost his honour for him, who would come for Juan's hand in marriage? He finished by being a bit tearful, saying that he had felt he had no choice.

My final reply was that he should have trusted me, despite everything. I would never have lost his honour for him because his honour was mine as well. This new life was a living death for me and he had chosen it. If I wanted to disgrace him, I could do so even now. At that he became silent; he looked down, unable to look at me crying.

I cried until there were no more tears left, loud or silent. Everything inside me had dried up and rotted away.

Chapter Eighteen

I REMEMBER that day so well that my own pain almost vanished at the sight. I had faced a lot in life within a short time but I never dreamt I would see such a day. Auntie Laila and I had been out for lunch and she had bought a few expensive items of clothing and make-up for me. I asked Jacob to take them out of the car for me as he was our driver that day. Uncle Majnu had asked him to accompany us because of the very short winter days; he didn't like us females to be out alone in the dark.

I told Fazo to take my things into my room. She had been my faithful maid who had been very kind to me at all times right from the first day of my wedding. She had almost become my friend.

'Begum... Begum, Laila Begum!'

'Fazo. Go and see what Majnu is calling me for. Tell him I'll be up in a minute. I'm tired. Jacob, oh Jacob, make the tea. *Now*, you useless man!'

'Oh, Jacob, bring some cakes and sweets for Kaashi. God, does she need fattening up!' She smiled at me. I smiled back at her.

'Auntie, come quickly. It's Uncle.'

'I know your Uncle called, Fazo. Tell him I'm going to quickly have my tea, then I'll come. Anyway, tell him to come down.'

'I don't think he can come down, Auntie. Sissy Kaashi, you come as well. Better still, Jaci, you come. We will need you. Come now. Hurry!'

The shouting from the top of the stairs became more urgent

and serious, almost as if she was gasping for breath. Jacob entered and said that we should go up now. It must be important, otherwise Fazo wouldn't call out. We both got up and while we climbed the stairs, Auntie Laila was still moaning, 'I'll sort you out, Fazo, if you've called me up for nothing.'

Fazo was standing by the open door of Auntie and Uncle's room. Her face was as white and as pale as a sheet with its colours washed out. Auntie pushed her aside, walking more quickly.

'Oh, my Allah. Oh, God, help me! No! No! Help him! Help, Jacob. Don't stand there with your ugly mouth open, showing all your blackened teeth. Shut your gob and get him down, you useless lump of fat.'

She grabbed his feet to lessen the burden around his throat. She kissed them continually, shouting curses at Jacob for not acting quickly enough and praises for her husband. The scarf was tied tightly to the curtain rod and the other end was tied around Uncle's neck. I looked on, absolutely shocked at the sight; no words came out.

'Child, phone Mirza!' she shouted.

I quickly phoned Mirza. I told him it was urgent and that his mother had called him and the others home right now. He said, 'What and why? Is it a matter of life and death?'

'Yes.'

I phoned the police and told them what I had seen. By the time I got back in the room, Uncle was laid out on the floor, and everyone was crying. The doorbell rang and Jacob went to open it. Soon the police and ambulance crew entered the room. They asked all of us to leave and we did. The police then came out and asked what had happened. I told them the day's events – how we had seen him hanging there. No one had been in the house but Uncle.

The door opened again. This time there was a body on a stretcher, covered with a white sheet. The brothers came into the house and Mirza looked at all of us. He took hold of my arms and shouted, 'Where's father?' His eyes were popping out in anger. His spit sprayed over my face as he spoke so vehemently.

'He's fast asleep on the stretcher.' I pointed. They all started to cry so loudly. All of a sudden they all fell on top of the stretcher so that it fell out of the hands of the ambulance men. All of them were weeping on top of their father like overgrown babies. Their mother started to curse them, telling them they would go straight to hell for dropping their father on the floor. No one was even listening.

Early next morning, relatives and friends all turned up. Everyone waited in turn to come over to Auntie Laila, especially the women. Each woman put her head, covered by a shawl, close to Auntie's; they cried in rhythm, almost in tune with one another. After a minute of crying, chanting, and reciting stories of all those who had previously died and the pain caused by their absence, they pulled themselves away and took off their shawls. They wiped their eyes and their runny noses in their shawls and then went and sat down somewhere.

Then they changed their mood from sombre to normal; they greeted others, asking about their family and news. My family also came and helped to serve food to all. A few families stayed the night as well. The men in the family organised the funeral and were out most of the time for the next couple of days until the funeral was over. As I sat amongst the women, some talked openly about why and how Uncle had hanged himself. Some covered their mouths and quietly spread the story.

Did someone do it to him? Who had made him so desperate that he would do this to himself? What had happened in the family? Could it be the new family member, or was it due to the one who no longer lived there?

Who was this 'one' who did not live there any more?

The men, along with Auntie, all went back to Pakistan with the corpse for the burial, which meant there was only Fazo, Jacob and I at home. It was so peaceful and relaxing, so unbelievably nice. This was the perfect time to bond a bit more with Fazo and to find out things about our family members that I didn't know about.

One evening, after dinner, I asked them both to tell me why Uncle hanged himself. They said they were not allowed to repeat the story but because I was a family member, I should know about the one who no longer lives with them.

Fazo explained that Raji was the only daughter and at the age of thirteen, whilst at school, she met a Hindu boy and fell in love with him. She was a Muslim and he was Hindu – it couldn't work. The parents didn't know the details but had seen them together. There were lots of arguments every day and then nothing. All of a sudden, everyone noticed that she was unwell all the time.

A couple of months went by and then one day she was taken to hospital and brought back in the evening. We were told that she was going in for a check-up because she was anaemic, but that evening when she came back, she wasn't herself.

She kept shouting, 'Murderers, killers! You'll go to hell. God will stick hot pins in your eyes for killing my baby. I curse you.'

Fazo continued. 'We realised then that she had been taken in for an abortion against her will. From that day on for at least a month, her boyfriend Karan and his family kept phoning and threatening and taunting the family. Raji was on their side so her mother stopped her going to school. Enough was enough. Then they sent her to Pakistan to stay with an aunt to learn how to be obedient.

'Before her sixteenth birthday, she was allowed back

home to England as long as she promised to behave. When she came back she seemed to be a changed person – quiet, shy and untalkative – unlike the Raji we knew. A couple of mornings later she started college and we started to see the old Raji again – mischievous, unpredictably extrovert and assertive. When she came home she always seemed to be tired and very sleepy. We were told to keep an eye on her at all times as she was drinking, smoking and taking drugs. It was hard, as she wouldn't let us enter her room. On one occasion, I went into her room without her permission, so she locked me in her wardrobe for half an hour. I didn't do that again.

'A few months later, she left home to live with her so-called friends. Uncle was becoming ill seeing her like this and then when she left he was devastated. He had got to the point of letting her do all this at home rather than away from home with her friends. He decided that at least when she was at home, he could see her and try to make her understand. Auntie kept telling him, "It's your fault. You have spoilt her yourself."

'This kind of lifestyle always has a sad ending and just before your wedding we got a call to say she was in hospital. Auntie told us that one of her so-called acquaintances made her take substances that had burnt her mouth, throat and her stomach. She would never be able to eat or drink again. She was being drip-fed and would never recover fully.

They also told us that she was almost six months' pregnant and they had no knowledge of who the father-to-be was. Uncle and Auntie didn't want the baby; they didn't want to look after it. It would be classed in our religion as a bastard because it would be a child born out of wedlock. The hospital wanted to keep her alive until the birth, as it was too late for an abortion and a bit early for a caesarean.

'The day that Uncle took his life was the day she lost her

life and the life of her unborn baby. He had deliberately sent us all out so he could go and see her in hospital. They told him that there was very little hope; just as he arrived home the hospital called. He loved Raji beyond belief. His eyes always twinkled when he saw her; he waited every day for her. You could say she was his life.'

Chapter Nineteen

TWO years had gone by since we had laid Raji to rest in England. Uncle was laid to rest in Pakistan but we missed both of them dearly in our hearts. We only talked about their good points and recalled only the fondest of memories. We had really thought that we would and could stay united. After all, the bad things that had happened, including my marriage, were all over now or accepted now.

Fate and death are both controlled by God and even if we want something, if fate or God has other plans then who are we to disagree or change them? It's simply not in our hands. Once again someone was knocking on fate's door without our knowing. We had grown up to believe this from the stories that Mother told us.

Nanny Ma, too, had spent hours every evening telling us the same stories that had been passed down by her parents. There was no radio or television and no books, so storytelling was an excellent way of ending the day. We were told to believe without question. A perfect example of this teaching was that no one has seen God and yet we believe that God exists – and that was that!

Since Nanny Ma died there seemed no need to go back home because there was no close family left. In this new family I had made a few friends and gained a whole lot of new relatives. Uncle Majnu's brother's only daughter was getting married and the family had asked everyone to come to Pakistan for the wedding. This is customary in our culture. Either you're rich and for the sake of the family name, relatives travel from around the world, or you're poor and their coming will ensure that the whole family gets a lot of money to help cover costs, or plenty of gifts, which go towards the dowry.

Either way the family also gets clothes for the occasion. These gifts were really not as great as they were made out to be but it was just the fact that something had come from abroad that gave it its importance. Members of the family made sure they told everyone that 'This item is from Mark's and Spencer and this is from Debenham's, and you know how expensive these are – they're designer!'.

All these gifts and the wealth would upgrade your status, no doubt, in the eyes of the locals but there were many more hidden agendas. You would expect a lot from the relatives when they came but a whole lot more when they left.

'Our roof is leaking. We have no money. Who will get it fixed?' 'You don't need to take those old clothes back, do you? No, leave them for me.' 'This radio is nice; we can't buy them here. You can get another one when you get back.' 'There is no television in our village. We want to be able to say our relatives have made us the first family to have our own.' 'Our other daughter is going to get married in a year's time. You won't be able to come back so soon.' 'Help us with that now and it will save you the trouble of coming back to burden us.' 'Our crop was bad last year so we need to buy new seeds.' And so on and so on.

The family produces lie after lie, all the time scrounging so much that they would rather send you back penniless and even steal the last piece of cloth from your back. So why is it that we go back for more?

This family was in the same situation as the rest. We had all prepared ourselves for this long journey back home, and for me, it was my first since my arrival in the UK. I was not nervous, just intrigued.

We could feel the heat as we stepped onto the tarmac at

Islamabad airport: hot, humid and very stuffy. I stood still to smell the warmth of the soil – it was as good that day as it had been all those years back. The welcoming guests all started to look exactly the same as one another; you repeated the same dialogue each time.

The wedding preparations had been made already, as we were only to be there for two weeks. The wedding had to start the week we got there so that we could enjoy one week of sightseeing.

Mirza and his brothers made sure that they got every extra thing the family ordered or wanted. They ran around doing the chores, organising this, organising that... and of course eying up all the local talent. Not that there was much compared to the talent they knew or had had. I do remember, however, that the house was usually full of girls.

The two bridesmaids, Lalli and Shaila, were there for a week. They were both very flirty and 'over the top' girls; if you gave them your hand, they would want to swallow it down before you could pull it back. They flirted at every opportunity; some people minded and others didn't, as some of the men were single and might make good partners for their daughters. All but one – Mirza.

It was the evening of the wedding day and there was a lot of hustle and bustle. No one knew where anyone was as there were just too many people. All of a sudden, there was a loud scream. Everyone stopped to listen – nothing. Everyone carried on. I looked over to the girls – there was so much noise coming from them. I went over to join them.

As I passed my bedroom, through the cracks of the wooden window shutters, I saw Mirza and his mother quarrelling. I stopped. They stopped. I carried on walking to join the girls. The music was loud and each girl was busy doing something. Lalli asked me when Maria was going to her new home. I asked her, 'What's the rush?'

She smiled and replied, 'No rush, *didi*. It's going to get dark soon and we've been looking for the red scarf for ages to put over the bride's head as she leaves. I've even sent Shaila to go and find it but she's been gone for ages.'

'I'll go to Maria's mother and ask her.'

I left and once again went by my room. As I did I felt inquisitive about what had been happening before. I put my ears to the window. I could hear quiet sobbing; the voice was of someone young but I didn't recognise it. I tried really hard to see who it was but the shutter was closed more tightly. All of a sudden the door opened, and Mirza grabbed my arm and dragged me quickly inside.

Now I really did get the bigger picture. Mirza stood against the door with his head down. Auntie Laila sat on the floor, sobbing. Shaila sat on the bed, clutching her clothes close to her, silent and terrified, with her make-up smudged and her hair messy.

'Please don't tell anyone what he's done. It would be better if you didn't know but you heard and saw everything. So it's better to unite at a time like this and hold this family together. That's what respect is, right, Kaashi?'

'Right, Auntie.'

I felt so disgusted. I could never have imagined that he would or could do anything like this. I think my curiosity got me into trouble that day. I wished I didn't know. I'm sure my face was pale with the shock as I started to walk towards the sitting room. I went in and sat in the corner at the back, away from everyone.

The drums started and in came Lalli and Shaila holding the red scarf over the new bride's head. The three sat together quietly. The bride got up and hugged her mother for the farewell ceremony. It was customary to shed tears as the bride was leaving. Lalli was crying and smiling but Shaila's tears didn't look like tears of happiness or tears due to the fact Maria was leaving. They seemed too personal, straight from the heart. I just stared at her continuously until there was no one left in the room, and then, she was gone.

'Still sitting there?'

'What? Oh, oh, yes,' I replied.

'Where did you go?'

'What do you mean? When?'

'*Didi*. The scarf.'

'Oh, yes... Er. Er... I forgot,' I said.

'Never mind. Auntie came and gave it to us, as well as the bad news.'

'What bad news? What do you know?' My heart started sinking.

She chuckled and with a big grin said: 'She told us girls that Shaila had fallen and Auntie came to her rescue. She even laughingly said what a sight she was. Trust someone to have an accident today. Thank God she wasn't badly hurt.'

I gave no reply – just smiled back at her. What would I tell her? About whom would I tell her?

Fancy that, just an accident, no one badly hurt?

Only scarred for life, that's all.

Chapter Twenty

SHAILA didn't return to the house the following week, even though messages were sent to her house. We had planned to go sightseeing for that week but I don't think anyone was in a mood to go. No one mentioned anything. Everything was as near normal as possible. The distance between Mirza and I grew wider. He explained how a jin (evil spirit) had overtaken his senses and why he had tried to rape Shaila, and I listened.

He even admitted that he had been wrong and should never have done it. He said that God would repay him for his sin in this life and not in the life hereafter. It was God who had sent his mother to save him from the evil temptation that he had been about to give in to. He strongly believed that God would pay him back for such a sin, especially because she was only fourteen. She was young enough to be his daughter.

His final words to me were, 'You have contributed to this sin I was about to commit. If you had made me happy, then I wouldn't have looked elsewhere for happiness. It's a wife's duty to give her husband happiness any time, day or night. You did not fulfil your duty.'

'You found others to make you happy in England. We were only here for two weeks. You could have waited. You can't blame me. After all, we have never ever shared this happiness anyway.'

Our flights back were confirmed for Saturday evening; we would arrive back in Edinburgh on Sunday morning. This would give everyone a day to recover and then it would be back to work on Monday.

Fazo had packed all our things and it was our last evening meal together with the extended family, so she made sure that I was looking extra special. It was customary for the men of the household to all go out together to the bazaar for the day, and return one by one in the evening. We, the women, had to wait until they arrived and only then could dinner be served.

That evening, everyone had come home except Mirza. It was eight o'clock and people were worried, as the normal coming home time was six thirty. Most of the men admitted to having seen him at Friday's lunchtime prayers but not after that. Auntie Laila was panicking; maybe she had her reasons. It was ten o'clock and still no Mirza, so still no food. Everyone was waiting together in the sitting room.

Some of the men had gone out to look, carrying lamps and candles in the hope of catching sight of him. I went to my room to lie down and told Fazo to wake me up when it was time to eat. I know it sounds really selfish but there was nothing that the women could do but wait inside, in the house.

As I sat on my bed, I remembered that only last night he had sat up with me while I was reading, hoping that I would put my book down and talk to him. The only thing he wanted to talk about these days was putting that awful incident in the past and effecting a reconciliation between the two of us. How could that happen? What would be different?

I had heard it all that night. The only thing he wanted to hear from me was that I had forgiven him. But how could I? It was too soon. Anyway who was I to forgive him? He did what he wanted – he was a man's man.

A woman had to worship God first and then her husband. So if he had nearly the same status as God in our culture and religion, who was I to judge him? This is what we have been brainwashed to believe. Men are superior and happy. Women are inferior and unhappy. Men, including Mirza, would remind me that a woman can go straight to heaven if she keeps her husband happy, but not if she displeases him, even if she's good to everyone else.

Thus a woman's main aim is to satisfy a man's habits and especially to respond to his sexual advances at all times.

'Yes. What is it, Fazo? Can we eat now? What time is it?' I spoke hurriedly but felt so embarrassed when I looked at her face.

As I looked round the room I saw that dawn was breaking; I knew it must be early morning. As for feeding my stomach, perhaps I should have thought before I spoke. To think of food at a time like this was insensitive. I had always been unpredictable but this time maybe I should have hesitated and thought a little before blabbing. I shouldn't always act on impulse.

'It's bad news, isn't it?'

'Yes, I'm afraid it is. Your husband has been found stabbed in the back. He was laid out in a field. Heartless people killed him. How could anyone stab someone in the back? That is a coward's way. What I don't understand – and the most bizarre of all things – is that people are saying it was Shaila's brothers, Dino and Murad, who did it.

'Why would people say that? She was here at the wedding and very happy. Why would her brothers do this? What reason could they have? People say that they have admitted to the killing but we must not repeat that. Why do they say this? Why aren't you saying anything?'

'You haven't really given me a chance, have you?'

'That's not the real truth, is it? Do you know something that I don't?'

'No, no. Go and do some work,' I said, then quickly left

my room and went into the main sitting room. Everyone, including the children, were all crying.

'Those bastards have killed Mirza. Heartless thugs! Killers! Murderers! How could they? Mirza didn't actually do anything to her. She was desperate and forced herself on my son. He was good; he fought her off. I helped her off him otherwise God only knows what might have happened.

'It's always the man that gets blamed and desperados like Shaila end up playing the victim. People give them money and sympathy. "Oh poor girl! Tut, tut!" "How awful!" Blah, blah, blah.'

'But, *chachi*, Shaila isn't like that. She's very simple,' said Naz, Uncle Mirza's sister's daughter.

'Simple! Don't tell me she's simple! Youngsters need to be seen and not heard. You were taught not to talk while elders are talking, weren't you?' Looking at her with great disapproval, Auntie Laila carried on. 'Your elder sister, Rani, was also simple. That's why she ran off at the tender age of thirteen. The other one – what's her name? Oh yes, Noor, oh so clean – had a different boyfriend every time we saw her. Your mother – didn't she run off with an Englishman? Yes she did! What a trollop! Then he found her hiding with her so-called black male friend in the local mosque. What were they doing in there? Praying? No. She didn't have the decency to hide elsewhere. Her dear father-figure husband, twenty years her senior! Why did she marry him, eh? He had to drag her out by her hair because she refused to come out. And as for your brother—'

'It's not all true, but yes, *chachi*, we get the picture,' said Naz, with her head down. Uncle Moosa, the eldest member of the whole family stepped in and asked everyone to be seated and to be quiet. He asked all the family members, including the workers, to come in.

Everyone gathered around. He explained that Shaila had

said that Mirza had tried to rape her and Auntie Laila had saved her. She told her family and they waited for the chance to pay Mirza back, God bless his soul. He was coming back from the bazaar alone. It was dark. They stabbed him and left him in the bare field where he could be easily found.

'People have questioned them and they're willing to admit to the killing because they have protected their sister's honour. No one will do it again. I have already made funeral arrangements for one o'clock this afternoon in our own graveyard. You're all going back to England tonight as already planned. I'll take care of things here. Now, finally, I'm only going to say this once, so everyone listen.

'No one killed Mirza – he died of a heart attack. That's it. We can save his dignity and his pride – end of story. If anyone breathes anything else, I will personally kill them, and that's a promise. Now, everyone go and get on with things.

'Abbas, my son, make sure the grave is befitting for your dear uncle and my beloved brother, Mirza, God bless his soul. Make sure all the arrangements are made perfectly yourself. We want him to go in a very dignified manner.'

Chapter Twenty-one

SAME room, same occasion – different man, different date. This time round, Sahel's parents came and visited a lot and so did he. He had grown up and so had I. Life had taught me a few lessons by now. They were sorry that it wasn't their son who had married me the first time, but no one could stop fate. They understood and sympathised with the fact that my first husband, Mirza, had died of a heart attack, leaving me a very young widow. Our wedding was never legal because we had never had a sexual relationship.

We had stayed together, sharing the same house, family and bed, but had remained like acquaintances rather than friends, even. They knew that I was treated well by everyone, especially the mother-in-law, but no one really knew if she was actually aware of the state of her son's marriage. Even though they all asked, no one got a reply.

The wedding day itself was quite a happy one, but it felt strange the second time round. It was not a lavish do because it never is on the second marriage. This time neither money nor love was an issue. This time the issue was about leading a normal, happy life with a man I could love who would love me back. After all, either you love someone and get married more like in Western society or you marry first and then grow to love the person as in the eastern world.

Peace and harmony lay at the beginning of our married life. It was very quiet compared to the last one. Soon after the wedding the parents moved abroad to where they normally lived and we had the house to ourselves. Sahel had a good job working for an engineering company as a consultant. His working hours were quite long and he was often too stressed and too tired to do much except on his days off.

We had a lot of good, quality bonding time as husband and wife, and yes, love did grow in our relationship. I know it seems unfair but although it wasn't Mirza's fault, I could never have had any feelings for him as a wife. Yet with Sahel the feelings grew strong straight away, even though I didn't want to love any man any more.

Because Sahel spent long hours at work, I had time to spend with friends and family. My family told me that Dinaag had also got married and as we both had shared some bad patches in our lives, I thought it might be good to get in touch again.

I had phoned her on many occasions when I was married the first time, but since I'd been single there had been no contact really. I never blamed her for not phoning me. I knew she was going through quite a lot herself.

I was really looking forward to seeing her; I wanted to see how she had grown and matured. I wanted to know what married life had taught her, as I think we all learn all the time, especially we females when we get married. It means giving all the time, taking less and less and trying to do all the things that we're expected to do and on time. There's no time to be selfish or immature any more.

I had already been moulded into a typical married woman in some respects while being married to Mirza; therefore things were not hard for me with Sahel. I thought Dinaag would have found married life easy as she was well used to taking care of everyone and everything in the house, fitting around others rather than the other way round.

'Hello, I've come to see Dinaag.'

'Kaashi?'

'Yes. Sorry, who are you?'

The lady in front of me was fully wrapped in black

clothes from head to toe including her hands. She had black socks on her feet. I could see the light in her eyes but there was a mesh cloth covering them. Automatically I started to smile, as we often called this strict Islamic type of clothing (the Hijab) a 'Ninja turtle outfit' and so anyone wearing it could be called a Ninja turtle. Dinaag lived with a Ninja!

She asked me to come inside into the living area. It was a very small, humble house. She shut the door behind us. All of a sudden, she took the big drape from under her chin and pulled it all the way back over her head. I stood shocked, but smiling at the sight. She smiled and then said quickly, 'Yes, it really is me.'

We rolled about in laughter. We started talking; she seemed a lot happier now than before. She seemed to be full of confidence, alert and at peace. She did admit that things had not changed at home but as soon as a marriage proposal had come along, she did not wait to see the prospective husband or find out anything about him. She said the only way to escape sexual abuse was to get out in a decent way, which for a girl, was through marriage.

Once married, she had found it hard to adapt at first because it all took place straight away – there was no time to get used to the change. Of course, the clothes had been forced upon her – she didn't believe in dressing in that manner. But there was no way out. This headgear, with the long, black coat, came as part of the wedding clothes. Women have to keep away from men. Once the door was shut, no man could enter without knocking and she couldn't go out without the clothes on, not even in front of her own family – only in front of her husband.

I asked her what her husband's name was. She replied that stating her husband's name was a sin as far as he was concerned. She had to refer to him as 'they'. He was superior to her, for she was a 'her'. He was not 'he' or 'him' but 'they'.

His name was Druff, but everyone called him Dodi.

She suggested we go out to a local café and talk, as Dodi would be home soon and so might his younger brother. They wouldn't come in because I was not covered. 'We will not be able to carry on talking,' she said.

So we went to the café. As we sat sipping our coffee, I was in fits of laughter so much so that it was almost a scene from a comedy. She was sitting comfortably trying to sip the coffee while keeping her face covered. How is that possible? She lifted the cloth a little and shoved the cup in the small gap. The more I laughed, the more she spilt her coffee.

Finally she pulled up the cloth and placed it on her head, saying, 'Damn it. Forget about being good for today! This is why I don't go out and stay indoors, undercover and away from all those who could not get tempted. By now laughing hysterically, she went on.

'Seriously though, Kaashi, do you really think that with a face like mine, fit for a horror movie, and a figure so fit that if a child blew on me, I would probably fly, is anyone really going to be tempted?'

'Have you ever rebelled against Dodi's wishes?'

'Yes,' she replied. She went on to explain that it wasn't worth the consequences. Both of them were like Hitler once Saif Ali, his brother, came home from work.

'And guess what? He's a butcher, and do you think that only men come into a butcher's? No. He sees women all day, half-naked at the shop! Anyway, I was getting dinner on the table. I found it hard trying to clean the forks properly so I took off my gloves; I had forgotten that he had come in. He didn't say anything, nor did I even think anything of it until, as they were both about to eat, I had to go into the kitchen to take off my veil and eat.

'Don't get me wrong. He does allow me to eat with him when Saif Ali isn't at home. Anyway he called me, "Bibi,

Bibi!" I put my veil on and ran to him. He asked me if my hands were naked. I said, "No."

'He said, "Remember. Please remember." I still honestly couldn't recall. Then he hurled the dishes from the table; they came at me like flying saucers. The shiny forks shone on the floor and the curry and rice were plastered all over me, the wall and the floor.

'I just thought, Oh well, they obviously don't want any food tonight! They both went out and I cleaned up.

'Another time, when serving food to him and his male friends, my glove got wet with hot curry, and, as a disobedient wife, I quickly took it off. Suddenly, in front of them, he took the serving spoon and hit me with it really hard. It made me put the glove back on straight away.

'The worst was when we were going to bed and I had to go to the bathroom again. I had already changed into my sexy lingerie, which I have to wear even if I'm cold. Anyway I was so sleepy and tired – after all, he had pleased himself three times already by then – I was so worn out that just for a split second I forgot the house rules. I went off to the bathroom and still half asleep, I came back and sat on the bed. Just as I touched the duvet I felt a harsh, warm slap on my thighs.

'I may sound naïve, but honestly I didn't know what had happened. I put my side lamp on and saw him looking at me furiously with his slipper in his hand. He stood there, naked, slapping me again and again, saying, "You will be cursed for flaunting yourself. There is a man in this house."

'I cried myself to sleep. Sorry. Am I boring you?'

'No, please carry on.'

'I think even worse was when I had to go to hospital because I was pregnant and I had to get myself booked in. Dodi went with me to insist that only a female doctor could see me at any time. After all, no man can see or touch me. A female doctor examined me and a female nurse checked me out. Then the doctor said that I needed to have an ultrasound that day to check on the baby. At that point it slipped my mind – we were both so happy that I was pregnant.

'We were in the middle of the ultrasound when I saw his face. I ignored it and enjoyed the view on the screen. We were standing at the bus stop afterwards. I told Dodi I needed to have something to eat or drink because I was feeling faint. He did not reply. There was a paper shop next to the bus stop.

I went in and bought an ice cream. I bought one for him too and offered it to him. He threw it on the ground. The sun was shining so brightly – it was the perfect day for an ice cream. I pulled up my veil and began to take the ice cream to my mouth. Suddenly he whacked my ice cream with his hand and it went flying onto the road.

'Then, with all his might, he thumped me on my back, saying how shameful I was. I didn't hear anything else as I lay flat on my stomach. I was in pain. Don't get me wrong. He's always saying what a good woman I am and yes, I am still waiting to get pregnant again. I am lucky to be alive, as I nearly bled to death. The ambulance came and took me from the bus stop. He just left me there to die. Who knows if I'll ever get pregnant again? Maybe God is cursing him for what he did to me.

'I know I still have a lot to learn to correct myself and be a perfect wife. Really he is a good man – just religiously strict. I think I've given you the wrong idea. I would rather have this life than the one I had before.'

For a girl who talked a lot, I had absolutely nothing to add, except tears for a very long time. Is sexual abuse worse than domestic violence? How does one decide? Why is it that women have to choose which one to live with? Why do we need to live with any? Why can't life be easy?

Chapter Twenty-two

WHEN two people live together in a house – one at work, the other a housewife – the housewife gets opportunities to indulge in friendships, especially if the neighbours are as interesting as mine were. The more time went by, the more attached to them I became. And who wouldn't? They were very caring. They used to ask me to come over; they gave me food and gifts, and a lot of news and gossip.

I didn't even have to travel anywhere. I could just pop my head over the fence and chat for ages. Many times it was almost like a scene from a soap or drama serial like *Coronation Street* or *EastEnders*. I watched and listened, but was still at a slight distance from these people, so, if I wanted to, I could switch off.

This household was normal in some respects. There were three women living in the house with one man. A lot of the time I could hear them fighting and yes, I mean physical activity: squabbling and shouting at each other with the slamming of doors. It was strange because I never heard the man shout at all. I hardly spoke to him but I often used to see him coming in and out of the house.

At first I thought the man was living with his wife and sisters. After all, that's what they had told me, so I believed them. Later on as I listened carefully to their conversation I realised that this household indeed was not as it seemed. There was no way of knowing, and, even though they accused each other of things, from what I heard it was all superficial stuff.

The man was near pensionable age; the eldest woman

was close to his age and the other two had at least a ten-year gap between them. The eldest was very senior to the second one. Not a day went by without someone shouting or slamming a door.

I got the impression that this household was one of the very few where male domination was by no means unchallenged. This household where the females ruled was very rare and also quite comical.

That day seemed like any ordinary day as I hung out the washing. I wondered what was happening next door as it was dead quiet. My thoughts roamed; why hadn't I asked what all the noise was about? I was only close to one of them, and didn't dare ask, but why didn't they just tell me? Anyway, it was really no business of mine!

I went up close to the fence and stood on tiptoe so I could clearly see over. Mr Alam was sitting at the end of the garden, smoking away as usual with his clothes billowing out like a white parachute. He noticed me and stared at me. I stared at him. He nodded his head slightly, giving me the same mesmerising look. These were the kind of eyes that could lure you to fulfil your desires and commit sins you would have no control over.

There was a glint in his eyes. His mouth was sealed but his eyes said a lot. I quickly swallowed the lump in my throat. The only thought going through my mind was, Thank goodness I have never met this man alone in a dark alley. I stopped looking at his eyes and looked at his six-foot long moustache. It curved under his nose and all the way down to the bottom of his face and then curved at the end as if it was gelled into place.

My toes fell flat on the ground but my curiosity pushed them back up again without my realising it. I saw Pinnee come out, crying and beating her hands against her head and knees. She was shouting, 'You bitches, bastards, whores, slappers, bloody prostitutes. I open-heartedly shared my husband with you and you repay me like this!'

He got up and with a roar like thunder shouted, 'Shut up or I'll shut it for you!' Her words stopped and the crying quietened but the beating carried on. I ran inside. Unaware of what to make of this I deliberately stayed indoors for the rest of the day. The thing that kept going round in my head was, 'shared my husband'.

As soon as Sahel came home, I told him what I'd seen. He said he thought perhaps I should go back to work as the nosier I became the longer my nose would get. He told me to stop playing the ignorant; these things happened all the time. Perhaps he was right: I was a bit too nosey and far too involved.

A couple of days went by and I tried not to stay in the garden for too long to avoid any contact with them. I felt that they were doing the same. How long would this last? What was *I* hiding? Nothing! As it was a Friday, 'parachute pants' would definitely be at the local mosque in his whiter than white gear, all shining except his face, which was the exact opposite, with eyes full of eyeliner and hair full of a whole can of oil. I went and knocked at their door.

'Hello, Kaashi *baji*. Come in. Where have you been? We haven't seen you for ages,' said Piya.

I entered to see a normal household, all three women cleaning. Pinnee asked me to come and sit down. She asked Piya, the youngest, to make tea and Nainee to get some snacks. They both went into the kitchen and she shut the door behind them. She knew why I had come.

She started to explain how she had been married at a young age but how, after a few years of trying for family, they had not been successful. This was Sahib's first marriage too, so it was hard to tell who was to blame or at fault. Naturally, the woman gets blamed and after a few years she gave up and told him to remarry.

'He said he could never divorce me because my parents were dead,' she continued. 'Where would I go? You see, it wasn't for love that he wanted to stay with me. He convinced me that with my permission, he would marry, but I was to remain his wife also. Asking my permission was a load of rubbish, as he'd already talked to potential parents-in-law. He married Nainee while I watched, trying to look happy.

'They were unable to have any children so they went to a private clinic. After a while, we heard that Nainee was expecting a baby at last. I asked him why we couldn't have had the same treatment, as I was longing to have a child of my own. Naturally he replied that he couldn't afford it again and promised me that this first child would definitely be mine.

'This was the first and last child for Nainee, as she has such a big mouth on her; she calls him by name and he doesn't like that. She talks back to him and he doesn't like that; he's not used to it. The crunch came when he told her that the first child would be given to me. She said that she and all her family would curse him if he did that – no other children would be born to him and God would send him straight to hell, dragged by his moustache.

'He's a man's man and as soon as she had finished, he slapped her – just the once, mind you. She lost her balance and the labour pains started. The baby was OK but the mother was never to have children again. Nainee hates me because of that.'

'As for Piya, well, he married her after announcing to both of us that even though he spent alternative nights between us two, he isn't fulfilled. It's what mid-life crisis does to men. When they're no good for anything they remarry. Piya was a desperate prostitute whom every man wanted but no man wanted for a wife. But my desperate Sahib Alam did.

'She has more rights with him and gets more money than us. She manages to leave her three children for us to mind while she goes out. Where? Yes, you know – shopping, and even more, window bloody shopping. Any excuse to get out of the house.

'That day, I realised what I am worth as the eldest wife. I should be treated like a queen, according to Islam. Instead I've become the pauper. I have nothing and he won't even divorce me so I can make a life elsewhere. You know, legally he isn't married to me; he didn't want to marry until I could give him children.

'He only carried out the religious ceremony so, in the eyes of Islam, I was his first wife. Of course a wife can never divorce a husband, only the other way round. I am almost like a slave, looking after their children. Look at those cows, acting innocent and nice in front of people. After someone leaves the house, that Piya starts dissecting them; she's backbiting all the time. She says I should do all the work as I have no children.

'No religion gives the right to anyone to practise polygamy, except in special circumstances, but men twist these religious laws to suit their cultural lives.'

So Nainee and Piya were not sisters but wives! Mr Sahib Alam was a polygamist. Who would have believed it? Dirty old man! No wonder we would hear Pinnee quoting dialogues from Indian movies like, 'Sahibiyan Alam, don't do this.' These are words taken from very famous romantic Indian movies. He the romantic and she the suffragette. Deep down inside she loved him dearly, otherwise there would be no way that she would recite passionate dialogues from romantic movies in a very poetic way. Did this Sahib Alam feel the same for Pinee as Shehzada Salim did for his Anar-Kali Kaniz in *Mughal-e-Azam* or was she just an emotional hanging on to hope?

Chapter Twenty-three

OUR neighbours remained the same and their story continued in the same manner. I would jokingly ask Sahel if he would ever want more than one wife. He always laughed and replied that one is more than enough. One woman could make a man's life. Two, however, could help to destroy it. 'You can only just take the nagging and pressure from one, let alone two,' he said.

He did however admit that circumstances could change. For example, if I couldn't have any children he was sure that his family would pressurise him into remarrying so his family name could carry on. He said that obviously he couldn't answer the question – would he obey them or not? Knowing him and knowing the male species within our culture, I knew that he would. Oh well, it's just as well that we did, or, rather, that I was able to have children.

I had always believed that when a person's partner dies they should always honour their love and life together and not remarry. Otherwise I felt that their married life meant nothing. Once again Sahel maintained it would depend on circumstances. I think all this means is that you do what you want at the time.

I took Sahel's advice and started to get a life of my own rather than try and live other people's lives for them. After all, I had my own appearance to preserve. Who would want a massive nose on a moderately charming face?

We'd moved to Wales and I was working as a trainee doctor in a hospital. For a Scottish girl, I had blended in well with the Welsh folk. How could I not? Both areas where I'd lived were rural, and medical college and hospital life weren't that different.

I never understood why I didn't acquire either country's accent. I looked, spoke and felt like a true English rose of London. I say 'English rose' because, for an Asian, my complexion was very fair.

Wherever you go you meet people of different backgrounds. Wherever I went I either took trouble with me or faced it myself, or got very clingy with people who were burdened with problems. Was this because I was inquisitive, assertive, nosey, or because I was a good listener? Or indeed is this real life in an Asian culture or is it a normal woman's life in every culture?

There weren't many Asians working with me at all at the hospital; there were only three others – two females and one male. The male was a very friendly guy, a happy-go-lucky person named Sami. He had come to Britain to study but was enjoying his time here very much. Even though he was a simple, humble guy, he believed in looking after number one and enjoying life to the full.

Selina was a bookworm who was always obsessed with books, but not medical books: books on beauty, hair and guys. What little time she had left, she spent on shopping for make-up and clothes. This meant that she had to scrounge money to get her through the day. Tomorrow was always another day for her. Because tomorrow never comes she was never really prepared for it: her work and observations weren't always in on time, her medical reports weren't satisfactorily completed, and so on.

She lived for her days off when she spent the entire day shopping or, rather, browsing. If she could get any male to show her the slightest bit of attention she would seduce him and then tempt him to take her out for a meal and yes, of course, she'd want a present by the end of the evening; in return she offered herself, in the name of 'fun'.

The most sensible and intelligent person was Tia. She was older than the rest of us and more of a mother figure than a friend, as she was always trying to give us advice. I don't know why she always tried to do this. Perhaps she had a lot of experience of life herself. No matter how happy she was she always had a sad look in her eyes – her face told us the opposite of what she was saying. Her face revealed a thousand emotions, although she had said nothing.

Tia had been away for quite a while and none of us knew why. I had naturally mentioned it a lot to Sahel, who always told me not to act on impulse. People who act on impulse sometimes make grave decisions, assuming what may be the truth, though it might not necessarily be anywhere near the truth. As for the look on her face, he said I was imagining it.

Huh, what did he know? He could never read between the lines. As for body language, he didn't have a clue.

Tia came back after three weeks of absence and it was nice to see her. She carried on as normal, but something just didn't make sense. How could she be away for so long without an explanation? I didn't mind people being abrupt with me so I plucked up the courage and asked what was wrong.

I told her that I cared and that was why I was asking. I asked why it was in all the years of our friendship that she had never lost that sad side. First she just denied it all, telling me that I read too much into it because I was an emotional person. Then she admitted that, like everyone else, she had problems but she thought I was too young to know or understand. Fine, I thought!

It was a cold evening and I was working really late. A few of us were still at work finishing off. At eleven o'clock I left the building and as I walked to my car, I noticed that the staff car park was nearly empty. I couldn't drive straight out because a car was parked in front of mine. I decided to reverse and take the 'No Entry' way out as it was shorter than going the right way out. After all, who would care at that time of night?

As I turned the corner I noticed Tia's car but she had left work a long time before. I got worried; I got out and went to her car. She was in there, excited, laughing, giggling with whomever was with her. She certainly had a companion who was pressing all the right buttons and reaching something that no one else had ever reached. I'd never seen her so happy.

Next day I asked her but I cunningly lied to get the truth out of her because I knew she wouldn't willingly tell anyone. I told her I'd seen what was going on although I hadn't really. She said, 'I told you that you wouldn't understand.'

For the next half an hour she sobbed bitterly without saying very much. Instead of her talking, I did instead. I told her about my first marriage. The more I told her, the more she cried. I knew her tears were flowing from the heart that was dearly attached to that sad face. There was so much hurt and pain in her sobbing. So many tears!

The lines showing her age became so visible because her make-up was half off. She was blushing red with rage and extreme anxiety and frustration. She looked at me with her panda eyes. I realised that her life must be very, very complicated: a whole lifetime of sorrow was reflected in those eyes.

It had all started when Tia was only seventeen. She, an Indian Hindu, had met Ahmed, an Indian Muslim boy, at school. They both fell in love but their parents became enemies, especially his, because Tia wouldn't change her religion for him; a Muslim cannot marry a non-Muslim. They eloped and got married.

This happiness was short-lived, as he showed his true colours sooner than she would have liked. He came from a very close family but now he'd lost it, and was left with no one but her. This caused him a great deal of stress. His bank account had been frozen as his parents no longer put money in it for him. He was a lost man.

He had no job, no money, no home – only a wife. This was not what he'd planned. Every time they disagreed his temper flared up and she was continually on the receiving end of his violence. Domestic, verbal, physical and sexual violence was always on the agenda but the timetable was not clear on when and where. He always said sorry when he had calmed down but he blamed her as well because, as he said, it was because of her that he had lost everything. He wanted her to shut up when he was angry.

She continued. 'To please him I took a job at a local supermarket. But I had to quit, because frequently I had to miss work because my eye wouldn't open up where he'd thumped me. Or I couldn't lift my arm properly because it was badly bruised by his hockey stick. Or he had raped me or tortured me by beating me for sexual pleasure.

'He said he was disgusted with his actions and that he wasn't normally like this; he didn't know why he'd become like this. The results of the physical abuse healed and I could cover myself up. But the verbal abuse stuck like glue in my head, so much so, that I had a nervous breakdown.

'All I know is that I woke up in hospital alone. How I got there, I didn't know. What I hadn't told the hospital staff, my marked body told. I stayed silent because I loved him still. The last time I saw him was when I was still in hospital. He asked for forgiveness.

'I refused. He said gently, 'I'll give you a divorce, divorce, divorce.' In Islamic law a man can just say 'divorce' three times and the marriage is officially over. All that remains is for him to carry out the formalities. A woman, of course, can never divorce her husband.

'Now, many years later I still love him and miss him. But to get over him I took another husband. He's a retired gentleman who worships me because he needs me. I need him to help me carry on and he needs me to look after him because he's disabled. I didn't get what I needed in my young life and I am now making up for it, I know, in a very bad, sad, twisted way.

'I know that I wear the trousers in the house and that was the only way I would have it. I take out my temper on Hossein and I know I'm wrong. I'm doing what was done to me but it wasn't my fault, nor is it his. He won't have long to live, I know, as he's frail. My abuse leaves him speechless.

'My time off last month was linked to Hossein; he had phoned Social Services to report my dreadful activities. If they believe him, I could be looking at a long jail sentence. From a small-town girl I've become a wretched witch. What will everyone say? Well, certainly not what you thought, right?'

'No. This story is the opposite of everyone else's. It happens to women, Kaashi, as we all know, but to men?

'Oh Lord, I'm a sinner.'

I had only one question for her: 'Why did you do this to him?'

'That's easy. The first year of our marriage was great, but as my mood swings and tantrums became more and more apparent, because of my depression, he said he had fallen out of love with me and into love with someone else. He was so close to divorcing me. I couldn't be brushed onto a rubbish heap again.

'Why couldn't he carry on loving me? How dare he reject me! He was idolising the other woman he wanted to marry, saying how understanding and patient she was. She was a giver, not a taker. Well, I thought, if I can't take, I can give – and I did. He has asthma, hypertension and has recently recovered from a major heart operation.

'He fell last month. I just helped him a little and now he's in a wheelchair! Oh, Lord! Ward off evil! Ward off temptation for I am a true sinner! Oh yes, by the way, I don't enjoy having all these men in my car but I'm slowly trying to use and abuse the men in our society the way that I have been. Payback time!

Crying even louder now with her head in her hands, she said, 'The good Lord will pull out my tongue, and tie it to a tree and then ask me to run to save my life. But alas, there's nowhere to go.'

If this payback was so sweet, why is it that she is not happy? Revenge is not really the sweet smell of success by any means. Are these the actions of a strong woman or the cries of a helpless, confused individual?

Chapter Twenty-four

THINKING back over my own life and the lives of other women who have come into contact with me at some point, I feel I've learnt a great deal from it all. The most important thing I've learnt is that, even today, male domination is so well established in women's lives and not just in Muslim women's lives, although more so in eastern societies than Western societies. In Britain, we've even had a woman, Margaret Thatcher, voted in as prime minister.

We have moved on to a better and fairer way of life in this country. In some communities, male domination still exists but it's a lot weaker than before. So why is it that women are second-class citizens? Even though I still speak before thinking – yes, I'm still impulsive – I will remain my own person and I haven't followed in my husband's footsteps.

There is a lot that I wanted to change in my life but at least I've taught my children how to live with a mind of their own – always listen to others but the decision has got to be yours. Don't ever be dominated by anybody, especially not by men. If you give them the hand of friendship, they feel they have a right to control you.

Equality has such a sweet meaning – two individuals walking the same path. Why is it that women can't teach their children to demand their rights rather than accept what is given to them as charity? Do men fear us? Are they afraid of our strength? I don't know. There are so many unanswered questions.

There are few answers, or is it that we don't want to make the change? We want to fit in and belong. Western women are very independent now, but the women in my culture still just say, 'Well, that's the woman's role.' The new generation, however, don't necessarily follow the old beliefs. They've grown up to be more independent; males are much more open to equality. But if you don't demand and aim high, you don't get.

When will we see a life without any verbal, physical and sexual abuse? I don't think it will ever really happen. It wouldn't be realistic to expect that, would it?

Auntie Marian tried all her life to keep the family together and accepted totally what life handed out to her. She still remains passive, even today, but as for my father, he's too old to be aggressive or controlling. I sometimes think that if my father had treated her better, she might have treated us better, maybe with love and compassion. Yeah, right – live in hope or, rather, in cloud cuckoo land. Well, at least *she* would have been happier, that's certain.

Dinaag went from sexual abuse to physical abuse. The domination was passed down to her own daughter who, from the tender age of one, had to dress in a burkha, covering her from head to foot. Orders came from higher up – no, not God – Dodi. He told her that her brain and all other women's brains were trapped in their heels. Every time she moves they either get lost or by the time the brain comes up to the head, it's too late and is of no use.

Dinaag's father died several years ago of a heart attack. Sohail, her abusive brother, was killed in a car crash as a middle-aged man. Even today, she carries on with her daughter in the way her husband intended her to do, but not so religiously.

Zara is still happily married to a very understanding man and feels happy that the sexual abuse was laid to rest there and then. Her abuser, Daanish, is a free man.

Shaila was blamed for her rape and so her brothers made

sure they married her off to any candidate – which turned out to be a much older man. She still lives with him and his eight children, and three of their own.

Hossein died soon after Tia's revelations; not long after, she fled the country. No one has heard from her since. Was her marriage to Ahmed a mistake? Was her marriage to Hossein an even bigger mistake? Did payback time really taste so good? Was the second marriage a good cover-up for the out-of-wedlock child she was pregnant with?

Hossein, a decent man, didn't suspect anything. This in our society is totally unacceptable; a child born out of marriage is a disgrace. Aman, the child's father, didn't know she was expecting the child. She didn't want him to know. Is this an intelligent, educated woman?

Sahib Alam is, unbelievably, still alive and kicking. Pinnee went to live with her brother because she needed looking after when depression kicked in, which affected her mentally and physically. Piya lives with Alam and their four children. As for Nainee, Alam bought the house next door for her to live in with her son. Sahib, even now, shares nights between the two women. He's still the king of both houses.

Auntie Laila passed away after having a stroke. Her kidneys packed up; dialysis was short-term and no donor was found.

Selina went to practise back home in Kenya and looks after her elderly parents as well. Sami has calmed down and married his girlfriend who is the mother of his child. His first girlfriend left him, taking the child she had by him.

Uncle Terry died a few years ago of Parkinson's disease and his wife, Auntie Libby, is seriously ill with a life-threatening illness.

Dhaani, my bridesmaid, was not a bridesmaid the second time round, and found a handsome partner for herself, and both sides of the family are very happy together.

Cousin Solomon died peacefully in his sleep a few years ago.

Fazo and Jacob both still serve the family faithfully.

Rahul, my eldest brother, lives happily in the Midlands with his small family and his wife's extended family.

Vinny and Rishab have remained stuck together like glue and share the same house and same business, and that's it.

The youngest child, Zubi, died at the tender age of thirteen, of a blood disorder. He's always in our hearts, but in our eyes he is nowhere to be seen.

Juan has always remained firmly and favourably in my heart and will do so from birth until my last breath. She's a part of me, of my mother and her mother. She has two children of her own and, after many years of struggling, has finally settled down with a reliable and stable man.

Zia and Zen, brother and sister, still live very close to each other with their families in Berkshire.

Zia has been the most sensitive of all the brothers and sisters. She has remained forever faithful and kind, responsive to everyone and everything. Whenever I ask her why she is too nice to people, she says, 'No one can be too nice. There isn't enough niceness to go round.' She's the only one with whom I've shared absolutely all my feelings.

Finally there's me: my birth as a daughter; my marriage to Mirza and then to Sahel – a wife twice; a sister to seven and a mother to five children of my own. Was my first marriage my mistake or someone else's? Or is it all in the hands of God? I remember the tears of silence that I shed as a baby, a child, a teenager, and a woman and through the struggle of keeping my marriage alive whilst teaching my children the right to equality, which went against my marriage and their father. But I survived.

Throughout this process, I wish that someone had heard me cry, heard my tears of silence. But no one heard. I do firmly believe that if my mother was alive, she would have done.

Chapter Twenty-five

MY life has not been perfect, but then, neither has anyone else's! They say that life is only what we make it. So what did I actually make of mine, and of my own children's?

I remain married to Sahel and we both enjoy our pension age: we love the freedom and time together. We haven't killed each other or had any extra-marital affairs.

We were both independent and have had successful careers. I haven't been a total devotee of religion, or so I've been told. If I had been I wouldn't have chosen to have only five children. Some of my closest friends used to say that we don't have the right to practise birth control because no one but God has the right to decide who lives or dies or comes into this world.

Financial stability and good health have meant that we've both enjoyed our children together. Our fine children have all shared in a success story of their own and so have not encountered any of the serious problems that my friends and I encountered. They've all grown up and moved to London where they're still pursuing successful lives today.

Our eldest is Kez, who joined the forces at seventeen. He was so physically fit and energetic that he definitely needed a career that was physically very challenging. He managed to meet all the demands of the job so that within a short period, he became a corporal. And he went on to higher things after that.

His main goal in life was to remain fit and promote fitness in everyone's lives. As an Asian, he's helped to recruit young blood into the most challenging work environment where the blink of an eye can mean life or death. He has faced it himself many times. Death doesn't frighten him, as he believes that to live as a hero is to die a hero.

He has grown and matured while travelling round the world, including war-torn areas – a true professional. These first-hand experiences have made him a strong person who respects people and life. He's the spitting image of his father, but their personalities resemble and differ too. His father is from the older generation; my son is of the new generation. He has always had a special place in my heart.

Moosa is the youngest of the children, but the opposite of his brother. He has no time for action as we know it; all his energy is devoted to his fingers as he's an information technology analyst. He's slightly shorter and slimmer than his older brother. He's an absolutely sharp, hardened City boy. He works in the City and meets new people every day. His communication skills are excellent and he has an eye for detail; one day, hopefully, he may find success like Bill Gates.

Saibaan is the eldest of the girls who, in her own right, is a success story. She's a designer who has gained her experience through working with the top designers of her time. She has a lot of charm and wisdom, and has a model's qualities. She's never taken up a career in modelling though, because she wants to remain a designer. Her smile is her best asset – it can warm even the dullest of days.

As a woman, she has always respected men and women equally and gets the same respect from her spouse; she's very respectful, as she's been taught in that manner. She would rather get hurt than hurt someone. Her spouse was uprooted from abroad but he has adapted to a life of harmony here with her. He has all the hallmarks of a typical Pakistani guy, but has transformed himself into a modern man of today. Even though Haaris was born and bred abroad, his thinking is very Western, an open-minded boy, full of charm and personality.

It's when he's upset that religion and culture become a big issue. His view is that women, including his wife, should be covered from top to bottom. Saibaan would never have it and they can argue all they like, there won't be a result. He then puts it aside and moves on. Strange as it may be, he comes from a family where six boys did everything, including running the house. They make a very handsome couple and are very jolly as well.

Rhea and Raaziya have a gap of one year between them and are both fine examples of Western society. Both of them push each other to the extreme limit and they both try to find the one thing that they can use to upset the other. Believe me, it always works, morning, afternoon and evening. Rhea wants respect, as she's older. Raaziya wants leniency because she's younger.

Rhea, a successful psychiatrist and counsellor, believes in studying hard to reach her full potential and it has paid off. She has always done things right the first time.

Raaziya doesn't believe in working hard but, because she's intelligent, sometimes she can get away without trying too hard. She's had so many narrow escapes. She's probably only recently learnt from them – a bit late, but better late than never. She always had the potential to be a doctor, a traditional career, but she took the easy way out and became a beautician, successfully running her own salon. If her best friend, Leanne, had stayed with her always, I think she would have been totally sane and sensible.

Neither woman is domesticated as they never had a need to be; you could apply the word 'lazy' to all three girls when they're at home. Rhea, sensible, sensitive and reasonable, has made a lot of great male friends, one especially – Vikesh. Our culture doesn't believe that someone of the opposite sex can be just a friend, but she firmly believes it's possible. And so far she has convinced us as well. Vikesh is a true friend and provides plenty of support.

As for Raaziya, well, she's genuinely a good friend and will cross all barriers to befriend those who are hers, which can lead her into trouble, not that that has ever bothered her. She's positively assertive but can, even at her age, give you a look that makes you reassess her attitude from assertive to oversensitive or aggressive.

Both of them are the exact opposites in everything. Rhea would stand behind, Raaziya in front. Both achieve results but in different ways. One is patient and convincing and the other spells it out clearly, whether anyone likes it or not.

How is it that my generation of women think so differently and yet I have managed to raise such strong females, who would never accept being dominated by a man? The men I raised also don't believe in dominating or suppressing a woman; they feel that the woman should be respected as she's the one who gives life. They even believe that nowadays it's women who control men, not the other way round. This generation has moved on, and thank goodness.

What hope is there for my generation? The more men tried to dominate me, the more I rebelled; not having a mother threw me in at the deep end. I swam – or maybe the younger generation would say that I drowned – I suffered so much. My marriage has not been blissful by any means, because if Sahel had had his way, I would be seen rather than heard, and I'd be fully covered.

As he progressed in life and his needs had to be met, he was happy for me to be assertive and strong, as long as I remained feeble and passive with him. In many respects, his values are backward. I had to fight every inch of the way to gain any freedom and rights for my children so they could grow up with free minds and not tread in their father's footsteps. I've struggled all my life to get equality and independence for them so they could make their own minds up. It was almost like wasting my married years rather than enjoying them, to some point.

He always had temper tantrums and always blamed me for them. 'If you kept quiet, I wouldn't need to get angry.' My life was like running a hurdle race – every so often I had to jump over an obstacle. I was a rebel and a bad one at that, but his problem is that he cannot admit that he is at fault. After all, everyone is entitled to their own opinion and no one is necessarily right or wrong.

My excuse? I had no mother. Maybe that's why I was strong enough to stick it out rather than give up. I don't know which is better.

My children witnessed all this first hand. They always thought I was rather passive at times and let things go, but they also knew that I was very strong-minded and did things assertively as well. They knew that I am myself but I have, as a woman living with a dominant man, been oppressed to some point. I wish I wasn't because I could have done with love and harmony, especially because I didn't get it in my childhood, but instead I got happiness from the children and anger and dominance from him. All I've ever tried to do is keep the family together and survive for myself and for them as well. And anyway, I firmly believe that I don't have the right to deny them of their father. Children are better off having both parents.

If I had to take this route again, would I? No, I would definitely not. But life holds no guarantees. Life has taken away the happy smile and rewarded me with a mask. After all, we are all actors, playing a role in our society. I wear it because I want everyone to see a happy-go-lucky woman. It's another way of staying positive and looking to a better future rather than an unhappy past.

I am myself, a woman who has shed more than her share of tears of silence.